PRAIS

BUILDING A BRAND THAT SCALES

"Jed provides CEOs with a practical branding framework and real-world examples to lead their teams in clarifying brand purpose, articulating brand promise, and codifying company culture. The resulting internal-external brand alignment accelerates growth by making and keeping a meaningful promise at scale. Alignment catapults organizations to top performance."

—CARINE STROM CLARK, Four-Time CEO
and Venture Capitalist

"In *Building a Brand That Scales*, Jed Morley takes the complex task of identifying, articulating, and expressing a brand down into consumable and orderly components that fit within a comprehensive framework. Not only does he make the process understandable and actionable, but with so many good stories, very relatable.

Jed's fundamental explanation of branding as making and keeping promises resonates deeply with me. I've had the opportunity to work with Jed on branding projects and have seen firsthand how his approach to building a brand that scales works. One rebranding project he led played a central part in our company growing from a small sideshow startup to being the leader in a new multibillion-dollar software category."

—GARIN HESS, Serial Entrepreneur;
Founder and CEO, Consensus

"As a founder or CEO of a software company, you've probably heard a lot about product-market fit—but what about your messaging? *Building a Brand That Scales* shows you how to apply that same mindset to your marketing with the Message Market Fit framework, helping you craft messages that truly resonate and drive growth. Jed has been a friend and a mentor to me for almost 20 years; I'm excited to see him share his insights with everyone now."

—JORGE MAZAL, Former Chief Product Officer, Duolingo; Founder, Outsmart College

"I love great models and frameworks—especially those that distill complex ideas into actionable insights. *Building a Brand That Scales* by Jed Morley is, hands down, the best I've seen on how to think about and systematically build a great brand. Morley doesn't just present theory—he lays out a structured, deeply practical approach that demystifies branding and makes it accessible to founders, leaders, and teams who want to create something enduring. His Backstory Brand Wheel Framework is a game-changer, providing a clear, scalable methodology for defining, articulating, and executing a brand strategy that truly resonates. If you care about building a brand that stands the test of time, this book belongs on your desk—not your bookshelf."

—MARK ABBOTT, Founder and CEO, Ninety

"*Building a Brand That Scales* is an excellent resource for leaders who want to create a brand that grows with their business. Jed Morley delivers a clear, actionable framework for developing a compelling brand story, ensuring alignment across teams, and driving meaningful impact. Whether you're launching a new brand or refining an established one, this book is the perfect guide to sustainable brand success."

—MARY MCCHESNEY, Chief Marketing Officer, Crucial Learning

"Jed Morley's *Building a Brand That Scales* masterfully connects brand purpose and company culture, showing leaders how to create organizations that consistently live up to their brand promise. His insights into crafting meaningful purpose statements and aligning teams around shared values offer a practical road map for leaders aiming to create lasting impact and exceptional performance."

—TOM SMITH, Coauthor of four *New York Times* bestsellers, including *The Oz Principle* and *Change the Culture, Change the Game*

BUILDING
A BRAND
THAT
SCALES

BUILDING
A BRAND
THAT
SCALES

HOW TO UNLOCK THE
HIDDEN VALUE IN YOUR
BRAND AND BUSINESS

JED G. MORLEY

FC

FAST
COMPANY
Press

Fast Company Press
New York, New York
www.fastcompanypress.com

Trademark Notice
The Backstory Brand Wheel Framework, The Backstory Brand Wheel Assessment, Message Market Fit, The Backstory Messaging Matrix, and The Backstory Messaging Funnel are trademarks of Backstory Branding. All other trademarks and registered trademarks mentioned in this book are the property of their respective owners. The use of any trademark in this book is for editorial purposes only and does not imply any affiliation with or endorsement by the trademark owner.

This work is being published under the Fast Company Press imprint by an exclusive arrangement with *Fast Company*. *Fast Company* and the Fast Company logo are registered trademarks of Mansueto Ventures, LLC. The Fast Company Press logo is a wholly owned trademark of Mansueto Ventures, LLC.

Distributed by River Grove Books

Design and composition by Greenleaf Book Group and Bill Chiaravalle
Cover design and interior figures by Bill Chiaravalle
Illustrations by Silwat Wisansak

Publisher's Cataloging-in-Publication data is available.

Print ISBN: 978-1-63908-119-6

eBook ISBN: 978-1-63908-120-2

First Edition

For leaders and teams who dare to build great brands.

CONTENTS

PREFACE

"Know ye not that they which run in a race run all, but one receiveth the prize? So run, that ye may obtain."

—*The Apostle Paul*

Coach Mike Thacker was no pushover. He always wore a whistle around his neck, and he wasn't afraid to blow it. His thick astigmatism glasses magnified his eyes, and his maroon polyester short shorts gave him an authentic early 1980s coaching aesthetic. Coach Thacker's no-nonsense approach commanded respect, so when he told us to run around the backstops of the Lakeridge Junior High ball field in our eighth-grade PE class, we did it. Only I did it a little too well.

The next thing I knew, Coach Thacker had recruited me to run the half mile, or 800 meters, on our junior high track team. That meant I had to run laps around our gravel track for the entire PE period the rest of that spring while my friends played softball and kickball. I always ran my hardest because I believed in doing my best, and I didn't want to blow it when it was time to race.

It Takes a Little More to Be a Champion

Our school's track and field area butted up against some neighboring backyard fences. One homeowner liked to lean over his fence like Wilson, Tim "The Toolman" Taylor's thoughtful neighbor on *Home Improvement*, and watch me run laps. One morning, he yelled some unsolicited advice to me as he watched me work out: "It takes a little more to be a champion!" I knew he was right, but I didn't want to hear it because it only added more pressure to my already high expectations.

These monotonous training runs gave me time to reflect on *why* I had accepted Coach Thacker's invitation. What was the point of running in circles every day? Was it the privilege of competing in nerve-racking track meets and squeezing out two laps as fast as I could against other runners doing the same thing? It didn't help that the half mile was always one of the last events of the meet. I sat in the shade, watching the early sprinters goof off on the high jump mats for the rest of the afternoon while I waited for my event. One question kept weighing on my mind while I waited: Would I have the courage to run through the wall of lactic acid pain that makes muscles feel frozen as I rounded the final corner and sprinted down the home stretch for the finish line?

I drew inspiration from watching *Chariots of Fire*, the movie that compares and contrasts two very different runners' motivations for competing. Harold Abrahams, a Jewish athlete, ran to make a name for himself and elevate his social acceptance and standing. Eric Liddell, a Christian missionary, ran to glorify God and spread the gospel of Jesus Christ.

My favorite part of the movie is when Eric Liddell's sister, Jenny, shares her concerns with Liddell that his running career could distract him and take him away from the ministry. To which Liddell replies,

"Jenny, I know God made me for a purpose, but He also made me fast, and when I run, I feel His pleasure." Like Liddell, I believe that if God has given you a talent, you ought to use it for good as an expression of gratitude for His gifts and to glorify Him. And the self-mastery resulting from the discipline of training and competing as a runner is an incorruptible crown no one can give you or take away once you've earned it.

It wasn't until I ran my first sub-two-minute half mile five years later during my senior year of high school that I felt like I fully developed my talent for running. Basking in the glow of that moment with my high school coach, Dave Houle, I felt deeply satisfied that achieving your personal best is worth the work and the sacrifice. My times were only good enough for sixth place at the state meet that May, which barely put me on the podium. But more importantly, it gave me a sense of commitment to always do my best and have the courage and confidence to take on other difficult challenges in life.

Coach Houle and I worked together toward that goal for four years. It was Houle who, years earlier, had encouraged me to write my split times on my bedroom mirror with my mom's lipstick (thanks, Mom) to help me visualize and internalize my running goals and develop the daily habits to achieve them. Those split times became my man-in-the-mirror accountability partner and a self-fulfilling prophecy.

He was the kind of coach who would be waiting for you when you finished a lonely long-distance training run. Having been a runner himself, he knew the value of having someone rooting for you when no one else was watching. For sprint workouts, Houle had us run sub-sixty-second 400s until we thought we would puke and sent us out together on fartlek group runs, where we took turns leading the way and drafting off one another for miles. And I wore Nike running shoes all the way.

There Is No Finish Line

An early Nike poster has a headline that spoke to me then and still resonates with me today: "There Is No Finish Line." The poster's image of a solo runner on an endless road is inspirational and unforgiving. It talks about the runner's high that serious runners experience, a feeling of being suspended in time and space, a feeling that you can run forever. Once you've visited that realm, you can never forget about it.

Between its innovative waffle shoes for training runs, nubby spikes for racing, and inspirational ads, Nike had my number. It was the only brand of running shoe I wanted to wear because I resonated with Nike's brand purpose: to provide innovation and inspiration for every athlete in the world (and if you have a body, you're an athlete). Even though I didn't know what a brand purpose was at the time, I could feel it in everything Nike communicated through its performance-driven products and motivational marketing.

Nike understood and shared the self-mastery aspect of my "why," and the brand became a vehicle for helping me feel something transcendent when I achieved my personal best. The Nike brand became the source of product innovation and emotional inspiration for helping me chase down that truth.

What's Your Best Time?

Warming up in the bullpen at a track meet is the worst. You've got butterflies in your stomach while jogging, bounding, stretching—and trying to make casual small talk with the other runners. The final race of my first year as a runner was one of my best. It was at a regional meet called Alpine Days, where every school in our valley tested their best runners against one another. In the bullpen that day, I asked an athletic-looking runner who was stretching out beside me, "What's your best time?" Of course, it was the same time as mine. I had gone undefeated in our dual meets against other schools, but we'd never run against one another before.

No matter how much you think you're prepared for it, the sound of a starter's gun is always startling when your integrity is on the line. I still thought of myself as my main competitor despite having a worthy opponent to draw out my best performance and vice versa. We broke away from the pack early, and I settled in just behind him, drafting like Coach Thacker taught me. We both held our positions through the first lap and a half. As we rounded the final turn, I surged ahead and caught him as we ran neck and neck down the straightaway. The wall met us one hundred yards from the finish line with paralyzing pain. With a last-second surge, I edged past him at the line, leaning in, with my parents looking on from the stands, my dad's signature whistle piercing the air. The blue ribbon was mine, and I was wearing my Nikes when I won it.

Just Do It

Nike's famous "Just Do It" slogan didn't hit the market until a year after I graduated from high school in 1987 and stopped running competitively. By then, Nike had already burrowed its way into my heart and mind, along with the hearts and minds of millions of other loyal fans, by linking its brand to the feeling of having the courage to rise above your fear, uncertainty, and doubt and do what is necessary to achieve something more. To this day, I still keep my Nike racing flats as a touchstone and reminder of what it feels like to catch up with your potential.

A Brand Is Not a Logo

In college, I studied graphic design, thinking I could learn to build great brands if I could just learn how to design an iconic logo like the Nike Swoosh. I soon learned that there is more to building a brand than designing a memorable logo. In grad school, Lisa Fortini-Campbell helped me discover the power of consumer insights and the need to get below the surface to understand why brands do or don't connect with customers on an emotional level. I learned principles for discovering and unpacking the underlying emotional drivers and motivations behind people's thoughts and behaviors in relation to the brands they love, including how to uncover and activate those strategic brand insights to build a strong customer following and successful business.

Working at IDEO, the global design and innovation consultancy, and witnessing its design-thinking principles, I saw the significant impact human-centered insights can have on creating brand connections and winning business models. The firm's empathy-driven culture informs and inspires relevant and unexpected solutions to people's problems that naturally fit into their way of life. During my time at other agencies and as head of marketing for various companies, I saw how hard it can be to create cohesive brand alignment when leadership teams hold conflicting opinions and chase competing priorities. Too often, they lack empathy for the people who actually use their products and services—and why those people buy them.

This book is dedicated to leaders and teams who are committed to building a brand that scales by setting their brands apart from the status quo and forming lasting relationships with their customers by consistently making and keeping a meaningful promise.

Think of this book as a coach who wants to help you achieve your personal best when it comes to building a great brand. The principles I share in this book come from over twenty years of experience, culminating in lessons learned from collaborating with dozens of businesses and brands at my brand strategy and messaging consultancy, Backstory Branding (Backstory), where we aim to build brands that live up to their promise. Our proven process consistently results in brand breakthroughs that accelerate growth and maximize the value of companies at exit. If your brand is stuck, underdeveloped, or undefined, this book is for you.

We've successfully applied these principles across industries, including accounting, affordable housing, ag tech, art publishing, beauty, consumer goods, construction, cybersecurity, dental, direct selling, e-commerce, education, electrical, employee benefits, energy, financial services, fintech, health care, hospice, life sciences, marketing agencies, martech, professional services, real estate, retail, SaaS, software development, solar, staffing, surrogacy, warehouse management, and venture capital. This book will teach you how to build a breakthrough brand of your own with clear concepts and practical examples for applying them.

CHAPTER 1

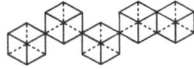

A DIFFERENT KIND
OF WHEEL OF FORTUNE

*"Sometimes you just stumble into something that works,
and here I am a quarter century later."*

—*Pat Sajak*

Some brands get big by getting lucky. They stumble into success and somehow manage to grow without much forethought. However, most brands that scale do so on purpose. Creating an intentional brand strategy gives you a much better chance of building a brand that can grow with your business, generate more revenue, and make a more significant impact in the world.

We've all seen brands that outgrew their initial vision. From the electrician who decides to add plumbing to his suite of services (electrical services—plumbing—and HVAC!) to Jiffy Lube's tacked-on Multicare moniker, it's better to build a brand that scales from the beginning than try to change your brand after you've already created a limiting anchor of association in people's minds that is difficult, if not impossible, to reset.

Brands that scale effectively teach their teams how to communicate their value in a compelling, consistent way. Their stories are focused and, at the same time, give them room to grow. Backstory's strategic branding process genuinely asks and anticipates what brands want to become so they can sustain their growth. They know how to articulate their value clearly and consistently at a high level through thoughtful brand messaging while simultaneously tailoring their messaging to each specific audience's unique wants and needs. They make meaningful promises and keep them at scale by building an intentional brand culture.

When I worked with Ben Peterson and Ryan Sanders, the cofounders of BambooHR, and helped them articulate their brand purpose—"We set people free to do great work"—we weren't simply coining a phrase; we were articulating their genuine commitment to creating a great company culture that lived up to their purposeful ideal every day. Because of Ben's and Ryan's deep commitment to live in alignment with their purpose, they built a brand that scaled from just thirty people when we wrote their purpose statement to over one thousand employees and over $100 million in annual revenue.

What Is a Brand?

At Backstory, we define a brand as the perception someone has of a particular person, place, thing, or idea. No perception, no brand. A brand could be anything from Birds Eye broccoli to Baroque architecture. Branding includes the thoughts and feelings we have when we think of a brand name and the reputation, value, and cultural currency it represents.

Customers determine what your brand is based on their cumulative experiences with it, and the branding process creates those experiences intentionally. You know you have a brand when your proper noun (i.e., capitalized) brand name becomes synonymous with the common nouns customers use to describe or search for solutions to their wants and needs.

For example, when you want a facial tissue, you say, "Please pass me a *Kleenex*." When you want to meet via videoconference, you probably say, "Let's make a *Zoom* call." When you want a blow-dry bar, you think—well, what do you think? What is a blow-dry bar anyway? As one of our workshop participants explained, "A blow-dry bar is where you get your hair blown out and styled without the cut and color of a traditional hair salon. When I think of a blow-dry bar, I think of Drybar. It's where my daughter goes to look her best for her forty friends' bat mitzvahs!"

Your business may own its brand name, logo, and tagline, but customers ultimately own brands because they decide what they stand for and, consequently, determine their value. You can *influence* what customers think of your brand, but you can't decide what it means to them. Everyone who works with you—employees, contractors, partners, and agencies—makes an impression on behalf of your brand, for better or worse. Defining what your brand stands for and providing your team with guiding principles for consistently communicating that meaning ensures everyone on your team can be an effective brand ambassador.

A Pragmatic Approach

Some branding philosophies use esoteric terms with mystical meanings that can be difficult for leaders and team members to understand or apply. Terms like "brand essence" can be useful in the hands of a sophisticated practitioner, but if your team members don't know what a branding term means or how to put it to work in their sphere of influence, what difference can they make with it? High-minded branding concepts are ineffectual unless your people internalize what they mean and make more decisions on brand. My goal with this book is to remove the mystery and ambiguity from branding concepts and make them as straightforward and practical as possible.

The Backstory Brand Wheel Framework

Branding is like painting the walls of a room with a vaulted ceiling. Other branding methods may take you a few feet off the floor but still leave the upper reaches of the room unpainted. The Backstory Brand Wheel Framework is a complete tool set, providing the scaffolding you need to access those hard-to-reach places and paint all the way to the top. This proven framework can guide your company through the process of getting its story straight inside and out to help you achieve and sustain the alignment required to build a brand that scales. Our four-phase framework is simple for nonmarketers to understand and implement and is meaningful to marketing professionals who want tools and inspiration to do their best work.

Phase 1 is Brand Discovery, the place where you uncover insights into your current and desired brand perceptions. In Phase 2, Brand Foundation, you clarify and articulate the ideas needed to communicate the five foundational elements of your brand story, including your brand purpose, brand position, brand promise, brand pillars, and brand personality. The focus of Phase 3 is Brand Expression, where you'll build on your Brand Foundation (i.e., brand platform) by defining the attitudinal and behavioral characteristics of your ideal customers, articulating the value you provide them, naming your brand, creating your visual brand identity, and defining the guiding principles for the visual, verbal, and experiential aspects of your brand. Phase 4, Brand Activation, aids you in consistently and correctly communicating your brand across all your customer touch points to drive brand performance and profitable growth.

The point of our framework is to simplify and systemize the branding process. Our straightforward brand definitions and methods have been designed to help executives and functional teams effectively develop a shared branding vocabulary and work together to achieve their brand goals.

Each section within The Backstory Brand Wheel Framework builds on the last, working from Brand Foundation at the center to Brand Expression in the middle to Brand Activation on the outer ring. The center of your Brand Wheel, brand purpose, never changes, and the four foundational elements that surround it rarely change. However, as

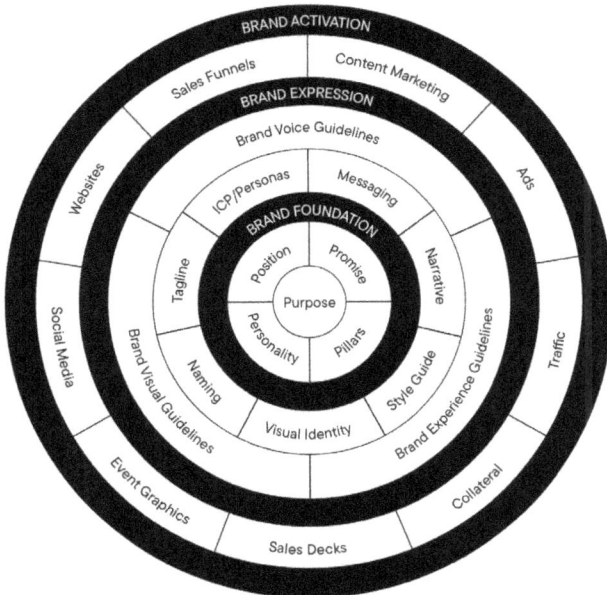

Applied Storytelling Brand Wheel concept used with permission.

you move out from the center, your brand elements evolve and change more frequently. In addition, the foundational elements in the center speak to all your audiences all at once while, on the periphery, the activation elements focus on targeted customer segments or audiences. I developed this framework while building my brand strategy and messaging consultancy at Backstory Branding, but you don't have to work with us to put the strategy to work for you. This book aims to help leaders and teams learn and apply the proven principles and best practices we've developed as another expression of Backstory's brand purpose—to build brands that live up to their promise.

I first learned about the brand wheel concept from my good friend and mentor, Eric La Brecque, the founder, chief brand strategist, and storyteller at Applied Storytelling. Eric's spirit of abundance and goodwill lit a fire in me to write this book, with the intent to share these concepts more broadly and build more viable brands. Fellow travelers and practitioners like Wayne Moorehead; my brothers, Nate and Burke Morley; and thoughtful clients and sparring partners like Ryan Wedig and J. D. Carter at Vasion have helped us round out and refine our thinking. As a result, Backstory's version of the Brand Wheel is a unique and effective model for building a brand that scales.

If you're wondering how my framework relates to other brand storytelling frameworks like Donald Miller's StoryBrand, The Backstory Brand Wheel Framework defines what to say in your brand story while StoryBrand teaches a story structure on *how* to tell it. Miller makes a great point—your customer is the hero of your story, and your brand guides your customer hero in successfully overcoming their enemies and reaching their desired destination. If you have a relatively straightforward story consisting of one or two audiences or one or two products, and an intimate understanding of your customers, the StoryBrand framework may meet your needs.

Backstory's framework and process are designed for brands with extensive product portfolios that serve multiple audiences with multiple offerings (products, services, and solutions that combine products and services). Simple, straightforward brands can use our framework, but it becomes increasingly useful for brands with multiple audiences and offerings. In contrast to StoryBrand's approach, The Backstory Brand Wheel Framework extends beyond brand storytelling to include other essential branding elements like brand purpose, brand position, and brand personality. And it includes defining your Ideal Customer Profiles (ICPs), customer personas, visual brand identity, brand culture or experience, and brand touch points.

I've written this book as a one-stop shop for your branding needs, a compendium that provides all the essential elements of branding and how to integrate them for building a brand that scales.

The Backstory Brand Wheel Assessment

Each element of your Brand Wheel may differ in its completeness and readiness to scale. If your brand has been around for a while, you may have already defined several elements in your Brand Wheel. If you're just starting out, have recently changed your product mix, or have introduced or acquired a new product or company, many of your brand elements may not be defined or may need to be refreshed. The rate of change varies by company, stage of growth, and industry.

To evaluate the current scalability of your brand, use our complimentary Backstory Brand Wheel Assessment for a summary of your brand's strengths and gaps. To take the assessment, visit www.backstorybranding.com/brand-assessment.

Upon completing a brief brand assessment questionnaire, you will receive a color-coded visual assessment via email reflecting the current status of your brand's various elements with defined elements in green, partially defined elements in yellow, and yet-to-be-defined elements in red. Your brand will be ready to scale when all the elements of your Brand Wheel are green. Turning all the aspects of your brand from yellow or red to green requires collaborative input from multiple individuals, teams, and departments. Teams that work together to turn all your brand elements to green create a shared sense of brand ownership, excitement, momentum, and alignment. Be sure to celebrate your progress and prioritize next steps as you turn certain brand elements green. Although the branding process is never-ending and requires continual renewal, appreciating how far you've come will help your team remain engaged and committed to doing its best work.

THREE TYPES OF BRANDING PROJECTS

Branding initiatives typically fall into one of three categories: new brand, brand refresh, or rebrand. The Backstory Brand Wheel Framework supports all three types of branding projects.

- **New brand:** New products, services, or companies clarifying and articulating their brand elements for the first time, including new brand names, visual brand identities, and brand audience and offering messaging.

- **Brand refresh:** Existing brands with defined brand stories and visual brand identities that are tired or outdated and need to be refreshed. In a brand refresh, the brand name remains the same.

- **Rebrand:** Existing brands making a big pivot, going upmarket, or changing their business model and positioning in significant ways may need a new brand name, as well as a new brand story and visual brand identity.

ANY INDUSTRY

We know from experience that The Backstory Brand Wheel Framework works for companies in any industry. Whether you're a business-to-consumer (B2C) company, a business-to-business (B2B) entity, a software as a service (SaaS) business, a professional services firm, or a nonprofit organization, using this framework and the principles we'll discuss in this book will help you build a brand that can grow with your company and communicate and command more value.

For example, Gabb, a B2C telecommunications company, first introduced a smartphone for tweens (kids ages ten to thirteen), allowing them to call and text a list of numbers their parents had reviewed and approved without open access to the internet. Building on the success of its first product, the company expanded its product portfolio to include a smartwatch and music streaming service. In doing so, the company recognized the need to clarify the foundational elements of its brand story to reflect its growing product portfolio. We worked with Gabb's founder and CEO, along with the company's leadership team, to clarify and articulate their brand purpose, brand position, and brand promise. We did a deep dive to better understand who Gabb's customers are, what they want, and why they buy. The insights we surfaced from our internal working sessions and in-depth customer interviews inspired a new brand position, "Safe tech for kids," for parents who want their kids to be safely connected as they expand their circle of friends and afterschool activities without giving them too much tech too soon.

In the SaaS industry, we worked with Rob Nelson, the founder and CEO of Grow (grow.com), a no-code, full-stack business intelligence (BI) software company. Rob asked us to help him clarify his brand story at three different points in his journey with Grow. Early on, we developed messaging to communicate the advantages and benefits of Grow's BI tools for small and midsized businesses that couldn't afford enterprise BI platforms, like Tableau and Domo. As the company expanded its portfolio of features and capabilities, we worked with Rob again to refresh and update Grow's more fully developed offering and brand story.

Then, shortly before he sold the business, we worked with Rob a final time to refresh the company's brand promise to reflect Grow's unique business model, which enables everyone on its customers' teams to make data-informed decisions within their areas of responsibility, not just the C-suite or executive decision-makers.

We worked with a seventy-five-year-old regional accounting and advisory firm called Tanner to differentiate its consultancy from the local offices of the national Big Four accounting firms—Deloitte, Ernst & Young, KPMG, and PricewaterhouseCoopers (PwC)—and local accounting firms competing for business in Utah's fast-growing Silicon Slopes technology market, among other industries. The process outlined in The Backstory Brand Wheel Framework helped us discover differentiators to set Tanner apart and deposition the Big Four and local competitors to make the firm relevant to the next generation of clients and highly sought-after talent. Tanner fully embraced the work and wove elements of its new brand story and visual brand identity into the workspace environment at both its flagship office and a new office to more fully immerse new team members in its brand.

ANY SIZE COMPANY

The Backstory Brand Wheel Framework supports branding initiatives across all four stages of business growth defined by annual revenue: early stage ($0 to $1 million), traction ($1 million to $10 million), scale ($10 million to $100 million), and hypergrowth ($100 million to $1 billion). The following are examples of how the branding principles and practices we cover in this book have helped companies at each stage take their businesses to the next level.

Early stage ($0 to $1 million)—DRYOUT: Romney Williams, CEO of Absorbits, engaged us to help him reposition his young ingredient brand to become the Gore-Tex of moisture absorption. In collaboration with Romney and his business partner, we interviewed individuals who represented key product categories that could benefit from the company's moisture absorption technology to provide more value for consumers. We explored problems these people face that Absorbits can uniquely address and tested different ways of describing the technology and its ability to pull moisture from the inside and outside of electronics and hard goods.

Based on the insights we gleaned from these conversations, Romney formed a new DBA for Absorbits, and we named it DRYOUT to quickly communicate the main benefit of the technology and help the company pivot into a new licensing business model. The new brand name made it easier for Romney to connect with manufacturers whose customers would benefit from the company's unique brand positioning and promise: "The only patented moisture removal material that prevents and rescues hard goods from moisture and damage."

It's important to note that young companies that haven't yet found product-market fit can gain valuable insights from clarifying their marketing messaging. The more you learn about the messages that resonate with your audiences and why, the more you learn about what business model and product elements resonate with them too. New insights into your business model and product inform your messaging and vice versa.

Traction ($1 million to $10 million)—Nano-Yield: By the time Nano-Yield engaged us, it had successfully applied nanotechnology to liquid fertilizers, fungicides, herbicides, and pesticides for commercial growers throughout the United States. Its groundbreaking approach packaged plant nutrition and protection in an unprecedented nano-sized package that more easily passed through plant walls to deliver intended payloads to improve crop yields and quality—particularly for specialty growers in the fruit, melon, nut, and vegetable categories. In contrast to the "more is more" mantra of traditional fertilizer companies, Nano-Yield's disruptive "less is more" approach required a reframe that would make sense to a skeptical "seeing is believing" market. Although growers were getting impressive results, Nano-Yield struggled to explain its new approach clearly, concisely, and consistently to distributors, wholesalers, and growers.

Our Brand Discovery and brand strategy approach allowed the company to position itself as the leader in nanoliquid technology for the agricultural industry. In addition, we worked with the founders to clarify and articulate the company's marketing messages (value propositions) for each of its core audiences, create a brand narrative to provide clarity and consistency across customer touch points, and write content for the company's website to bring its story to market and activate it.

Scale ($10 million to $100 million)—Crucial Learning: The four founders of VitalSmarts—Kerry Patterson, Joseph Grenny, Al Switzler, and Ron McMillan—are master researchers, teachers, and authors specializing in creating an effective company culture in which leaders and team members can have hard conversations, improve accountability, and facilitate change while preserving healthy working relationships. The books they authored and the training programs they built and facilitated—including *Crucial Conversations, Crucial Accountability, Influencer,* and *Change Anything*—became bestsellers within the learning and development (L&D) industry.

As the company grew and looked for new revenue streams, it licensed content from other best-selling authors, like David Allen, who wrote *Getting Things Done,* and Charles Duhigg, author of *The Power of Habit*, to develop new L&D training courses based on these popular books. The company's hybrid content portfolio made it challenging to tell a cohesive brand story—based on content titles alone—to marry its classic VitalSmarts content with its newly acquired titles and offerings. In other words, it took the company too long to explain what it did for customers and partners.

Using principles from The Backstory Brand Wheel Framework, we collaboratively found a path forward to leverage all the equity of the company's classic content and expanded portfolio. By rebranding VitalSmarts to Crucial Learning, we helped the business reframe its position and perception in the L&D industry as offering the most crucial and essential content for the most forward-thinking leaders regardless of who authored the content.

Hypergrowth ($100 million to $1 billion)—Lucid Software: Lucid Software already had ten million users when Dave Grow, the company's CEO, asked us to help his company clarify and articulate why people buy the company's flagship product, Lucidchart. The goal was to equip the company with new insights into why people buy Lucidchart within different departments across enterprise companies to make it easier for Lucid's marketing and sales teams to sell enterprise-wide, annually recurring SaaS licenses instead of individual employees buying it on their own.

Working alongside the company's product team, we interviewed dozens of Lucidchart customers from various functional areas across large customer companies. We dived deep to understand each customer segment's unique pain points and the features, advantages, and benefits of Lucidchart that solved those problems. The insights we surfaced from these conversations informed the company's brand or company marketing, product strategy, product marketing, sales, and client success motions.

Based on our research efforts, the Lucidchart team articulated audience-specific messaging to address the unique pain points for different disciplines throughout a company, including engineering (software development), IT, operations, product, and sales. In addition, Lucidchart built a horizontal messaging framework based on universal jobs to be done that almost any company would appreciate, including improving processes, optimizing organizations, visualizing technical systems, and replacing Microsoft Visio. Lucidchart's matrixed approach to communicating the value of its offerings enhanced the company's ability to articulate its overarching value and audience-specific benefits. As a result, the company was able to sell more enterprise software license deals and create better alignment among its marketing, sales, client success, and product teams. Today, Lucid Software's expanded visual collaboration product suite supports over sixty million people worldwide who use Lucidchart, Lucidspark, and Lucidscale.

Applying These Principles to Your Business

Throughout this book, we will define the elements of The Backstory Brand Wheel Framework and explain how to apply them to your company's brand-building efforts and growth strategy. Our systematic approach will allow you to build your brand and business by consistently communicating the value of your services in words, images, and experiences that resonate with your ideal employees, customers, and investors and help create your desired brand perception. Knowing how to express your value makes every marketing dollar work harder.

BRAND DISCOVERY

*"Insight perceives, intelligence understands,
intellect comprehends, wisdom knows."*

—Matshona Dhliwayo

BRAND DISCOVERY

Branding is a gift. Can you think of a gift someone bought for you that really hit the mark? A thoughtful gift that made you feel understood, appreciated, and valued? A gift that made you wonder how they knew? One of my favorites was a Livescribe pen and notebook gifted to me by a friend who noticed I take notes in meetings. The Livescribe pen records what's being said in the room and links it to your handwritten notes. Using the pen, you can tap notes you've written to hear the recording of what was being said at the time you took them. It's a remarkable system, and it was a remarkable gift because I never knew my friend had noticed my propensity for taking notes.

Of course, giving the perfect gift is even better than receiving the perfect gift. As Will Guidara, former co-owner of Eleven Madison Park—once named the best restaurant in the world under his leadership—reminds us, the most meaningful gifts don't have to be expensive. I gave a pair of Fiskars scissors to a woman who lived in a tiny apartment with barely any space to spare. It was a thank-you for participating in an ethnographic interview I conducted on behalf of a client in the creative DIY industry. The scissors were from the Fiskars booth at a trade show tied to the research project and had her name engraved on them. When she received them, tears welled up in her eyes. "This is one of the most thoughtful gifts I've ever received," she said.

The same skills required to be an effective gift giver are behind building a brand that scales. Those skills include being observant, perceptive, and insightful, as well as following through when it comes to understanding and acting on what people want and why, even if they don't seem to know for themselves.

In the movie *Groundhog Day*, Bill Murray's character wakes up to relive the same day over and over until he cracks the code on what his love interest, Andie MacDowell's character, wants. At first, he selfishly manipulates the people in his repetitive life to get what *he* wants, but eventually, he has a change of heart and uses his unique perspective to learn the pitfalls and preferences of the people around him to help them get what *they* want.

Similarly, the Brand Discovery process uncovers insights into who your target customers are, what *they* want, and what is in *their* way. Acting on these insights unlocks your customers' hearts, minds, and ultimately, wallets. Showing them you understand their problems and pain by creating and clearly communicating elegant solutions that solve their problems in emotionally satisfying ways is the essence of Brand Foundation and Expression. Finding the ways to convey and communicate the value you've created for your customers is the work of Brand Activation. When you get all these elements right, persuading customers to prefer and purchase your brand becomes much easier. Learning how to uncover and activate insights into what your customers want and why will make you and your team more effective brand builders.

The first phase of The Backstory Brand Wheel Framework is Brand Discovery. This phase focuses on understanding your current and desired brand perceptions and determining what gaps exist between them. Finding these gaps informs your brand strategy by identifying the words, images, and experiences needed to create your desired brand perception. If your brand reality is strong but your brand perception has fallen behind, this is the perfect opportunity to apply our framework to close your brand gap. Building a brand that scales requires you to first build a product and experience people want. You've got to have good brand reality to have a good brand perception. Working through each phase of the branding process will help you identify and close any brand-perception gaps thoroughly and consistently.

Four types of insight inform brand strategy: company insight, customer insight, competitor insight, and creative insight. Great brands are born where these insights intersect. The activities in Phase 1 surface all four kinds of insights. They include conducting internal and external in-depth interviews, along with completing a brand audit and competitive analysis of the market landscape. These activities help you gain a more informed perspective and uncover the insights needed to close any gaps between your current and desired brand perceptions with an effective brand strategy that defines the right words, images, and experiences.

CHAPTER 2

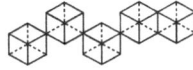

IN-DEPTH INTERVIEWS

"The best way to observe a fish is to become a fish."

—Jacques Cousteau

T he first step in Brand Discovery is interviewing individuals who have valuable insights into your current and desired brand perceptions. These in-depth interviews should include one-on-one conversations with your company leaders and customers who can provide meaningful and diverse perspectives into your brand and business in context of the competitive landscape. Like a doctor who uses an MRI to see a patient's problem from multiple points of view, talking with people who have different perspectives helps you gain a holistic understanding of the current state of your brand perception relative to what it aspires to be. Good interviews come from selecting and curating a group of insightful, opinionated, and articulate participants. Each should be willing and able to discuss what they think and feel about your brand and category and, most importantly, *why*.

No category is too familiar, obvious, or banal to yield brand breakthroughs that go beyond the superficial and, in turn, inspire great branding; however, the more differentiated a brand is, the better. For a software company serving the dental industry, I interviewed patients from a successful practice who told us about the positive differences those doctors made in their lives. One woman we interviewed talked about how her nutritional deprivation as a young child in a Nazi concentration camp compromised her teeth and oral health for the rest of her life. The effective treatment she received from her periodontist over the years meant a great deal to her, especially the empathy he expressed for the difficulties she had to deal with from her lifelong dental health issues. In appreciation for his kind and compassionate care, she gladly shared her story with us.

In contrast, another interview participant from this same practice, a gentleman who happened to be a psychiatrist, interestingly, wouldn't allow me to see into his heart and mind beyond superficialities. He was closed to the idea of sharing his feelings and refused to ladder up, so his interview was shallow and didn't unlock any insights.

Interviews with industry pundits proved fruitful for the dental company as well. A successful dentist and consultant I met at an industry conference shared how, when he was new in his career, he mistakenly thought of his patients in terms of how much money they could pay him—a profit-driven point of view. Eventually, he shifted from seeing his patients through that profit-and-loss lens to seeing them as real people with real hopes, dreams, and fears. A practicing Hindu, this enlightened leader explained that when he made this shift and started seeing his patients through the loving lens of his spiritual third eye, he showed appreciation for their humanity and treated them with genuine kindness, concern, and caring. In response to making these meaningful connections, patients opened up and started sharing stories with him about their cats and dogs and everyday life experiences. Connecting with his patients on a human level not only opened up enriching long-term patient relationships but also built a multimillion-dollar dental practice for this man by giving his patients trust and confidence to accept and buy his recommended treatment plans. His practice prospered when he saw his patients as people and built genuine relationships with them that went beyond building a business pro forma.

Some interviews that appear to be rather ordinary on the outside turn out to be a geode revealing multifaceted insights once you crack them open. We worked with a client who designs and manufactures ruggedized LED lights for two-story trucks and heavy construction equipment for the earth-moving and mining industry. After completing internal interviews, we interviewed customers from four continents, including a product support and sales representative based in Elko, Nevada. He was yelling on the phone to make his voice heard above the roar of his Ford F-350 flying down the freeway for an 8:00 a.m. appointment with a customer at a gravel pit jobsite.

He described his customers' pain points, which included struggling to switch out broken truck lights. Safety policies require production to halt when lights fail in the field—a costly problem given that a single hour of downtime can cost tens or hundreds of thousands of dollars depending on the size of the operation and the material being hauled. Despite the consequences of downtime, some truck manufacturers design their lights for obsolescence by putting them in fragile housing that breaks before customers realize the promised life of their LED lights.

The sales representative from Elko insightfully recommended that our client put their lights on service trucks—at the client company's expense—so reps could demonstrate the superiority of our client's lights as the trucks drove back and forth across acres of jobsite territory. He explained that doing so would demonstrate their superior light output and create a stir among competitive and performance-minded truck drivers who always want the latest and greatest equipment. It was a great idea the client hadn't considered. He made a compelling case from real-world experience that these in situ product demonstrations would drive bottom-up demand for lights that cost a little more to purchase initially but save clients money from a total cost of ownership perspective.

Our friend in Elko was a little rough around the edges. The language he used was plainspoken, a little colorful, and grammatically incorrect at times. But that didn't really matter. The important thing is that he was insightful, articulate, and opinionated; he'd had unique experiences with our clients' products and was definitely not shy about sharing what he'd learned about them in the field. He got his ideas across effectively and provided new concepts that contributed to creating and activating an effective brand strategy for our client.

Sometimes subtle asides and anecdotes from interviews inspire brand messaging and make all the difference. When interviewed, an ex-military customer of a cybersecurity company client called SecurityMetrics said, "They have my six," meaning our client compensated for his blind spot—the vulnerabilities of his business's security system that he could not see. His insight and explanation inspired us to develop a brand mantra to sum up our client's brand promise in only seven words: "Never have a false sense of security." Given the many products our client provided and the audiences served, what had been a wordy struggle to summarize suddenly became crystal clear. The new brand mantra, combined with a thoughtful, audience-specific messaging framework, helped the client tell a simple, coherent story spanning all its audiences and offerings. Being able to encapsulate and communicate its value proposition in a more compelling way helped the company significantly grow its business.

Asking Expansive Questions

The most fundamental skill to develop and apply in conducting effective interviews is to ask thought-provoking, open-ended questions. The goal is to invite the people being interviewed to open up and share more, not shut them off with simplistic, yes or no questions that drive the conversation down a dead end.

You can practice this skill when you check in with your significant other or kids at the end of the day. The types of questions you ask make all the difference. For example, saying, "Tell me about your day," invites conversation, whereas "How was your day?" invites a solitary one-word response. And asking clarifying questions in response to their answers to your initial question keeps the conversation going and deepens your understanding and appreciation for them and their unique experiences and perspectives. Similarly, an inviting approach to conducting in-depth interviews yields additional layers of insight and leaves the interviewees satisfied that the time they spent with you was worthwhile. We've even had interviewees thank our clients for the opportunity to talk with us because they found our questions and conversations so interesting.

The Brand Ladder Method

You can improve your interviews by focusing on the interviewee's purpose or reason for their answers. Discovering a rich "why" vein of golden insights to mine becomes more predictable and repeatable when you use the Brand Ladder Method. You may have heard of the Five Whys technique where you ask someone up to five times why they think or feel a certain way to understand the underlying desire or motivation behind why they do what they do. Although this approach can certainly produce some insights, the Brand Ladder Method consistently yields more impactful and actionable insights than other methods.

The Brand Ladder Method operates on four levels of insight: features, benefits, feelings, and values. Great brands communicate and connect with their customers on all four levels. A *feature* is an attribute or function of a company's product or service. A *benefit* refers to what a feature does for customers and—in the case of B2B brands—their businesses. For the Brand Ladder Method, a *feeling* is what it's like to experience that benefit, and a *value* is how it makes life better from the person's or the company's perspective.

In his 1984 presidential reelection campaign, Ronald Reagan's team worked with pioneering pollster and political consultant Richard Wirthlin, who used the Brand Ladder or Value Map, as it's sometimes called, to identify the issues that mattered most to American voters that year. Wirthlin correctly identified voters' concerns about their safety and security against the Cold War threat of Russia and found an opening for Reagan to distinguish himself from his opponent, Walter Mondale, on this values-driven issue.

Reagan's campaign leveraged this insight by working with legendary adman Hal Riney, among other advertising creatives, to create a nuanced but effective TV commercial called "Bear." The thought-provoking spot resonated with voters because it laddered up to an emotional level and helped set Reagan apart. The copy Riney wrote and voiced in the ad alluded to the looming threat of Russian aggression and helped reinforce the perception that Reagan was the better candidate for checking and, ultimately, dismantling it.[1]

Hierarchical Value Map: Reagan-Bush '84 *(August 1984)*

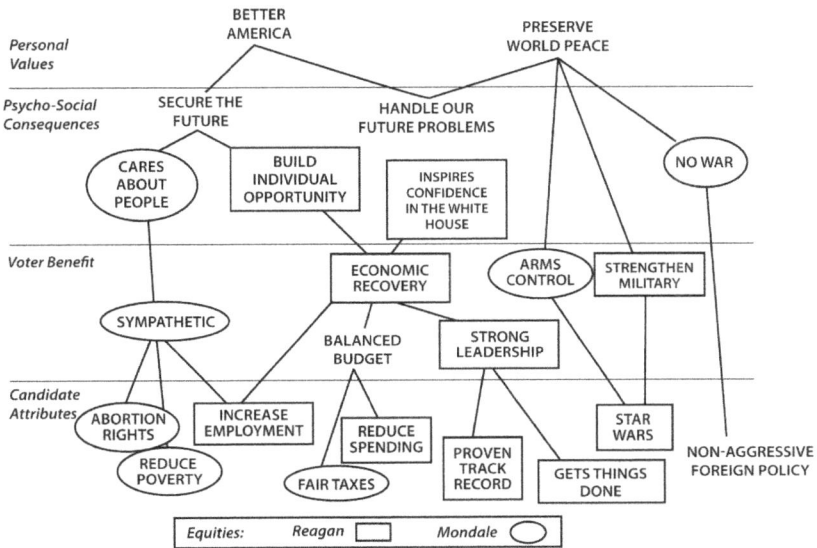

BUILDING YOUR BRAND LADDER

Four seemingly simple questions can help you build a brand ladder that unlocks strategic insights into your customers' wants and whys. I learned these questions from a talented protégé of Richard Wirthlin and am passing them along to you in service of helping you become a more gifted giver. Surfacing and activating these insights can enhance your natural branding gifts and intuition. Communicating on all four rungs of the ladder—features, benefits, feelings, and values—will allow you to connect and communicate with customers logically and emotionally, as Nike did with me as an eighth-grade 800-meter runner, creating a lifelong brand affinity.

- **Features:** Of all the things that set this brand apart, which one matters most to you?

- **Benefits:** What are the benefits of that feature, and which one matters most to you?

- **Feelings:** How does having that benefit make you feel?

- **Values:** What is important about feeling that way?

This four-part progression of questions can give you a decisive competitive advantage by unlocking insights that tilt customer preference in favor of your brand and motivate customers to act on those preferences.

WHY DO YOUR CUSTOMERS BUY?

Earlier in my career, I once worked on the Cricut personal electronic cutting machine, which became a national brand revolving around a tool customers used to make professional-looking projects, ranging from signs and posters to birthday cards and cake decorations. The company had one of the top infomercials at the time and was expanding its sales reach through big-box retailers. Buyers at these sophisticated channel partners wanted to know whether the business could sustain long-term interest among customers or if it was a one-hit wonder. The business had clearly struck a chord with customers. However, when the intuitive founder of the company stepped away from the business's day-to-day operations, the new team wanted to know why customers were buying the Cricut so they could keep the success story going and expand on it.

Using the Brand Ladder Method, I conducted in-depth, coast-to-coast interviews with customers who bought the Cricut. The interviews uncovered significant insights into the persuasive and motivating drivers behind the Cricut's stellar sales growth. Based on these insights, I built a framework that deconstructed and helped explain why the

Cricut brand and business experienced such tremendous success and why customers were so invested in it.

As it turns out, the Cricut resonated with customers from across the creativity continuum. They all embraced the brand's best-selling product but for different reasons. These customer segments ranged from creative beginners who carefully followed the company's step-by-step recipes for re-creating predefined results to power users whose free-flowing imaginations generated ideas of their own for creative projects—they just needed an easy-to-use tool to bring their endless ideas to life. The genius of the Cricut was that it met each customer group where they were on the creative continuum and enabled them to express their creativity in an emotionally rewarding way.

The company tapped into a big market by developing a system that supported a broad range of creative ability. It even inspired customers to form self-organized meetups. These Cricut jam sessions included gatherings in project rooms the company provided at its retail stores, as well as larger events held at local hotels across the country. At these gatherings, customers would spend entire weekends making Cricut projects together, sharing ideas, and building a sense of connection and community as they celebrated one another's creativity. These customers took pride in their Cricut creations and relished the compliments they received when they shared them with family and friends, which further validated their creative identity.

The customers I interviewed for the Cricut project told me how frustrated they felt by other creative enablement tools that were too expensive or difficult to use, including the Singer sewing machines that had provided a creative outlet for their mothers. One woman talked about trying to sew a blouse and being unable to finish it because the sleeves were too difficult to complete. She'd hidden her unfinished project in a drawer, an artifact of an unfulfilled promise from a brand of a bygone era and a missed opportunity to fulfill her desire to showcase her creative abilities.

Other interview participants talked about feeling creative when they were young children as their teachers and parents lovingly asked them to tell them about the pictures they drew in elementary school. "It's a horse, Mom!" they would explain as their parents attached the artwork to the fridge door at home. However, being unable to draw a realistic-looking horse in middle school became a social liability, and gradually, because they didn't draw well, they stopped thinking of themselves as being creative.

The Cricut tapped into the insight that adults who can't draw still have ideas for creative projects. This accessible machine ignited and rekindled their creative confidence and gave voice to their inner creative child. They just needed a tool to help them express creative ideas in ways that looked professional, reflected well on them, and communicated just how much they cared about the recipients of their handiwork.

Using the Brand Ladder Method produced insights that opened up new opportunities for the Cricut to connect with its customer love groups. It gave the company's sales executives a new way to tell their story to buyers at big-box retail chains, and it inspired ideas for additional products to extend and build on the Cricut's success.

BEYOND THE LADDER

Of course, conducting in-depth interviews using the Brand Ladder Method isn't the only way to surface consumer insights, but in our experience, it offers the most marketing ROI on finite time, money, and energy, and that's why we use and recommend this approach. Diving deep with individuals who represent several different customer segments can help clarify the issues that matter most when it comes to understanding why your customers perceive your brand the way they do and where you could take those perceptions from there.

Other qualitative methods, like hedonics-driven ethnographic research, can generate valuable insights and information, but they tend to be too time-consuming and resource-intensive for many companies. Focus groups can provide lots of feedback but often work best in responding to a hypothesis or concept informed and defined by insights gleaned in advance from in-depth one-on-one interviews. Surveys are good at generating surface-level information and converging on the best or most preferred option within a known set of variables. The following tables provide additional information about various qualitative and quantitative market research methods, including pros, cons, and considerations.

MARKET RESEARCH: QUALITATIVE METHODS			
Description	Focus Groups	In-depth Interviews (IDIs)	Ethnography
Details	• 6–14 participants • About 1 hour or more in length • Effective in an informal setting to help participants feel comfortable	• 1 participant at a time, 8–25 total in a study • 30 minutes to 2 hours long • Conducted face-to-face or digitally	• Many varieties, from 1–30 participants • 1 or many households
Pros	• Better ideation (people build on ideas of others)	• Useful for sensitive topics	• In-the-moment data • Rich in context and response material

continues

MARKET RESEARCH: QUALITATIVE METHODS			
Description	Focus Groups	In-depth Interviews (IDIs)	Ethnography
Cons	• Results can be biased because of a desire to hold to social norms.	• Requires rapport to allow a person to open up, understand emotions, and hear an honest take • People may feel pressured, and conversations may be less natural.	• Can be intrusive, depending on the method • Can be affected by observer bias
Considerations	• Watch out for dominant personalities, groupthink, and aversion to different views.	• Make sure you aren't influencing the conversation with your personal opinions or biases; positive and negative feedback are equally welcomed.	• Keep in mind that people may change their behaviors when they are being observed; it's important to avoid biases.
Techniques	• Laddering (value based) • Beyond talking (images, mission-based activities, role-play drawing) • Projective techniques ("find a picture to describe this," etc.) • Cocreation (create new content or innovations with a customer)		• In situ observations • Shop-alongs (and drink-alongs and you-name-it-alongs) • Self-ethnographies, mobile ethnographies

(Source: Matt Madden, Marketing Professor, Marriott School of Business, Brigham Young University)

MARKET RESEARCH: PRIMARY QUANTITATIVE METHODS

Description	Typical Survey Questions	New Product Development	Segmentation	Branding
Details	• Capturing demographics, psychographics, behaviors, satisfaction, etc.	• Various methods to test new product attributes and evaluate market opinions	• Creating unique persona groups to target	• Brand equity, brand tracking, brand positioning
Pros	• Research ties directly to actions • Relatively straightforward process	• Develops new features and products • Simulates new product launch	• Helps you understand your customers and prospects • Provides you with a guide to future marketing	• Allows you to understand and affect the perceptions people have of your brand
Cons	• Can be expensive • Potential for poor-quality data and fraud • Difficult to write a useful survey	• Requires in-depth customer and category knowledge • Best if preceded by qualitative research	• There is no "right way" to segment • Quantitative segmentation can be data intensive	• Branding is easily misunderstood • Doesn't make up for a poor product
Considerations	• Questions should have a clear purpose in mind • Avoid writing questions that are confusing or biased	• This method is used to test consumer reception to potential products, not to have consumers come up with new ones for you.	• Segmentation can be done based on a variety of factors, including demographics, psychographics, and behaviors.	• Branding is much more than a logo and a style guide; it's the perception someone has of a particular person, place, thing, or idea.

continues

MARKET RESEARCH: PRIMARY QUANTITATIVE METHODS				
Description	Typical Survey Questions	New Product Development	Segmentation	Branding
Techniques	• Basic tables • Stat testing • Correlation and regression	• Conjoint analysis • Concept test • MaxDiff	• Cluster analysis • Buy existing data groups • Create your own data cuts using LTV or other simple but useful metric groupings.	• Longitudinal tracking • Regression • Perceptual mapping • Brand narrative • Content marketing

(Source: Matt Madden, Marketing Professor, Marriott School of Business, Brigham Young University)

Pound for pound, in-depth interviews (IDIs) punch above their weight; they're the best way we've found to quickly and affordably produce substantive insights that get below the surface and give you a competitive advantage by revealing underlying factors driving customer perceptions and behaviors. In your interviews, you will definitely want to ask more questions than the four essential questions within the Brand Ladder Method. Additional questions that bring customer insights to the surface include the following:

- What comes to mind when you hear our name?

- What would you use if our brand weren't available?

- How would you describe our brand to a friend or colleague?

- Who are our biggest competitors?

- How do we win against them?

- How do they win against us?

- Who is our brand for?

- What is our brand's superpower?

- If you were hiring our brand, what would be its job description?

- If our brand were a person and they knocked on your door, who would be standing there when you open it? Describe them to me.

Interview Guidelines

Having completed hundreds of interviews for dozens of companies in diverse industries, we've found that following some simple guidelines can make a big difference in making interviews more valuable. Keeping these guidelines in mind can enhance your investment of time and energy with minimal added effort and resources.

THINK FIVE AND FIFTEEN

Generally speaking, completing five internal and fifteen external interviews provides sufficient insight to inform most brand strategies, assuming you have three to five customer segments. Consider doing additional interviews if your brand has a highly diverse customer or user base or if some of your products and services are relevant to small subsets of your audiences only. We recommend completing two to three interviews per customer segment to see patterns emerge. As marketing guru Geoffrey Moore defines it, "A segment is a group of people who buy for the same reasons and talk to one another"—groups of people who join the same online forums, attend the same trade shows and conferences, subscribe to the same podcasts and social media communities, and follow and engage with the same thought leaders.

BE SELECTIVE

Be sure to select insightful, opinionated, articulate participants who bring diverse perspectives to the discovery process. Being insightful means they deeply understand the subject matter as well as customer needs, motivations, and behavior in the context of the competitive landscape. They can explain *what* is happening and *why*. Opinionated implies they have strong opinions and aren't afraid to share them. Articulate signifies their ability to put their thoughts and feelings into words. One-word answers won't do. If someone likes playing hard to get when sharing their thoughts and feelings, select someone else. They've got to be openly willing participants. We're not saying they have to be well spoken in terms of proper grammar—colloquial language can add valuable color and texture to the conversation. But they do have to be able and willing to explain what they think and *why*.

Don't settle for mediocre or redundant conversations to satisfy political or other considerations. If you're obligated to include certain people who won't add much value, increase the number of interviews to compensate for what they lack, or provide a survey allowing for input from more people even if it's shallower than the interview process affords. Advocate for curating a collection of thought-provoking and substantial conversations to yield new insights and inform a thoughtful and differentiated brand strategy.

DO YOUR HOMEWORK

Prior to the interview, gather as much information as you can about the people you're interviewing and the role they play in the brand's buying process. Talk to other members of your team who are familiar with them, use Google and LinkedIn to read about their professional background or personal interests, and read and review articles and social media posts that mention them. Gathering basic contextual information beforehand preserves valuable interview time for nonobvious, hard-to-get information and enables you to be conversant about their business and industry or lifestyle and ask more insightful questions within your limited interview time. The more you know about the people you're interviewing, the faster you can build rapport and naturally invite them to be more open with you.

GET THEIR NAME AND A BRIEF BIO

For business-to-business brands, asking participants to introduce themselves, including a brief description of their role and responsibilities, provides a vital understanding of them and the unique perspective they bring to the discussion. Capturing this "station identification" information helps attribute who said what when reporting the findings and recommendations from your Brand Discovery work. Having a cross-section of perspectives is critical to lending credibility and context to your ideas.

PRETEND YOU KNOW NOTHING

We've found it helpful to pretend you know nothing about the industry or topic going into an interview and that you ask the people you're interviewing to assume the same. That way, you won't miss out on new insights they may have shared with you had they not thought it was something you're already familiar with. Remember that it's just as important to hear how customers and key opinion leaders (KOLs) talk about an issue or solution as it is to understand what they think about a given topic and why. The best brands speak to their customers using language that reflects and resonates with their worldview and culture. Interviews are a great way to gain a more intimate understanding of how your customers think and talk about what you do.

BE PREPARED TO OFF-ROAD

Preparing a written interview discussion guide specific to your brand and business is a good idea, but it's equally important to remain open to pursuing promising ideas in the moment. Being ready to off-road will help you recognize opportunities to ask clarifying questions, pursue surprise topics, and tug on loose ends to unravel unexpected insights that might reveal something new and significant. Side trips can fuel crucial findings and recommendations that make all the difference. Keeping your ears attuned to listen for asides, anecdotes, and after-thoughts from interviewees may seem off script at first but can provide valuable detours that shed new light on a familiar topic or unlock an entirely new frame of reference or greenfield opportunity.

BE COMFORTABLE WITH QUIET

If an interviewee is slow to respond to a particular question or says "That's a good question" and pauses, be prepared to let them reflect for a minute. During these quiet interludes, find your inner Zen and resist the temptation to interject and fill the void. Being comfortable with silence while still being present instills confidence in the person with whom you are speaking. Remaining quiet is a vote of confidence in them. Staying focused and not becoming distracted with alerts, notifications, and tempting text messages—especially on a Zoom call—allows them to feel respected and supported; they're more likely to trust the process as you patiently give them space to find the right words to express their thoughts.

ASK JUST ONE QUESTION AT A TIME

A common pitfall in interviewing others is to try to get too much information at once. Whether it's due to a lack of decisiveness or an attempt to clarify a complicated concept, some interviewers tend to ask long, multifaceted questions that create confusion and interrupt the flow. You'll get more relevant answers if you let respondents focus on answering one question at a time. Set your interviewees up for success by breaking up more complex ideas into their component parts. When people feel confident, they're more relaxed and articulate, and that's what you want. A good interview feels like a thought-provoking conversation, not an IQ test or inquisition. Facilitating an effective interview leaves participants feeling glad they took the time to talk with you. Well-crafted interviews leave people feeling like they learned something new based on your insightful questions.

GUIDE THE DISCUSSION

Some interview participants unleash word stampedes right out of the gate, responding to initial questions with a torrent of pent-up thoughts, analogies, or stories that can smother the flickering conversational flame and burn through valuable time without saying much of anything. Other times, especially for technical topics, the conversations can be quite dense and detailed. This is like the difference between skiing through fluffy, dry powder and heavy, waterlogged snow. Slogging through wet snow is much harder and slower than swishing through powder.

Although interviewing someone who is overly talkative is better than the alternative, it's ultimately *your* interview. *You* are responsible for navigating the narrative and taking it where it needs to go to unlock breakthroughs you can harvest on behalf of your brand and business. Do not cede control to an interviewee. You've got to guide the topics of discussion so they align with your learning objectives.

One way to do this is by leveraging what they've said and building on it. Using their words and finding out what those words mean to them is like scaling an indoor climbing wall. The first few footholds and handholds lead you up the wall along a thematic color line. Wisely choosing a multilayered concept or theme as a point of entry can create a unique path that takes you from obvious table stakes information to new ideas that could crack the code to your entire brand. Having a discussion guide to back you up if you run out of free climb handholds is like having a belay line to fall back on. Exploring multiple themes or pathways across a series of diverse conversations helps ensure you aren't limited to just one way forward for your brand—and you won't miss out on finding a new route to category leadership no one else has discovered.

TAKE TRIGGER NOTES

Jotting down brief notes during interviews is a good practice as a thought starter and trigger to aid your recall of noteworthy ideas or anecdotes. However, trying to capture verbatim notes in real time during an interview interferes with your ability to be present and slows the organic rhythm and flow of the discussion. Of course, recording interviews with permission from participants or using an AI tool to capture notes digitally can be helpful because it makes them immediately and consistently searchable. Handwritten notes require the extra step of transcription and can be difficult and time-consuming to incorporate into final deliverables and presentations.

DON'T SETTLE FOR SATURATION

It's not uncommon to hit a saturation point with certain questions in a particular customer segment when you're a few interviews into the process. When you're no longer learning anything new, it's time to change things up and ask new questions. Give yourself permission to explore new topics in pursuit of delivering more value to your company and customers rather than being beholden to a predetermined list of questions you've thoroughly addressed. Also, recognize that each interviewee will know aspects of some topics and use cases better than others. You've got to make the most of every individual's unique experience and knowledge with the goal of getting good coverage across all the questions from your portfolio of participants in aggregate.

HAVE THEM CLARIFY WHAT THEY MEAN— IN THEIR OWN WORDS

Ask participants to explain the meaning of the definitive terms they use in their own words. "Definitive" here means words that summarize a feeling or represent a core concept. Double-clicking on their vocabulary words is essential to understand the meaning these words hold for them beyond a rote dictionary definition. Don't be afraid to ask them to define words that, on the surface, seem self-explanatory—even if they get a little annoyed at you for asking them questions that appear to have obvious answers. You may be pleasantly surprised at the underlying meanings people attach to specific words, given their one-of-a-kind life experiences, points of view, or even misunderstanding. If you don't take time to unpack the meaning behind your customers' words, you might miss subtle nuances or sizable shifts in meaning that could make all the difference.

We traveled to Fargo, North Dakota, to find out what growers (farmers) thought of our ag tech client's software at an agriculture industry trade show in the Fargodome. When we asked them what they thought about our "cloud-based asset tracking" software, they told us "cloud-based" made them think of literal clouds (not SaaS software) that block the sun, and "asset" made them think of financial services, not the trucks and equipment we had in mind. When we explained that the software tracks trucks and equipment on smartphones, tablets, or computers, they said, in so many words, "Why didn't you say so?"

Reflecting on this experience, we realized we'd used an investor-oriented message for a farm owner or operator audience. This mistake was understandable because when we developed the minimum viable messaging with our client's input, their thoughts were flavored by their focus on raising investment capital. Based on this feedback, we created a new iteration of our messaging for the company's next sales event at the Potato Expo in Anaheim. We generated much more interest and engagement there, avoiding a messaging mismatch.

For Havenpark Communities, a company that owns and operates manufactured home communities, I interviewed a resident at one of their properties in the Midwest who explained she wanted to live in a community that respects her. When I asked her, "What does respect mean to you?" She looked at me quizzically as if to say, "Doesn't everyone know what respect means?" So, I calmly clarified that I wanted to make sure I understood what respect means *to her*. Though somewhat perturbed, she explained, "Respect means treating people how you want to be treated." She went on to share that the previous community manager failed to consistently enforce their community rules. He looked the other way when her neighbor had friends over on the weekend and parked their cars in front of her driveway so she couldn't get her car out to drive to the grocery store. For her, respect meant she wanted the community to hold her neighbor accountable for upholding the rules and, at the same time, validate her worth as a person. Her insightful comments, along with others like it, inspired us to position the brand as "caring communities across America" based on its commitment to living the Golden Rule for community managers, residents, and Havenpark employees: Treat others as you want to be treated.

DON'T CORRECT THEM

During an interview, if someone misuses or mispronounces a word and says something like "imply" when they should have said "infer," don't mention it. If someone says "personal" instead of "personable," you won't gain anything by pointing it out. Let these types of inconsequential infractions ride if you know what they meant to say. Your goal is to make people feel comfortable and confident in sharing their underlying desires, attitudes, beliefs, and behaviors. That won't happen if they feel self-conscious because you've pointed out a mistake they've made, however well-meaning your intentions. Also, don't disagree with someone's opinion or argue with the insights they're giving. They're already being vulnerable in sharing *their* truth; let them share it freely and be curious about why they're saying whatever they're saying without judging it.

RECORD THE INTERVIEWS

Recording all interviews is essential because you never know when someone is going to say something magical. Like the fizzy sound of cracking open a Coke, effervescent insights can evaporate in mere seconds. And good luck getting them back because people struggle to recall and repeat what they said just moments ago. It's not just *what* people say but *how* they say it—their word choice, emphasis, and intonation. Be sure to let participants know you're recording the conversation and get them to acknowledge the recording when they introduce themselves. It can be as simple as saying, "With your permission, may I record the call?" If it's a video conference call, Zoom has a feature that notifies participants you're recording and won't let them access the meeting without accepting it.

In a few minutes, most people forget about the recording and openly share what they think and feel as you demonstrate genuine interest in what they have to say by being an attentive listener. Recording interviews allows you to be present and attend to the conversation at hand without worrying about missing something. It also ensures you can review valuable insights and accurately attribute them to the right people. The quality and production values of the interview recordings don't need to be perfect, but they do need to be clear enough to transcribe accurately.

TRANSCRIBE THE INTERVIEWS

Transcribing your interviews makes it easier to review and remember who said what and how many interviewees said the same kinds of things, not to mention providing empirical data in support of your ideas. AI-enabled transcription tools are rapidly matching the quality of human transcription services while delivering results at a fraction of the cost and time. It's not uncommon to pay a premium for time-stamped transcription, though this may not be necessary. Using Zoom or another video conferencing platform gives the advantage of capturing compelling video clips to share in your presentations, literally bringing the customer's voice—and body language—into your conversations with your team and decision-makers.

CODE THE INTERVIEWS

From creating in-depth Microsoft Word documents and Excel spreadsheets to using social science tools like MAXQDA, coding, or indexing interview transcripts produces textual evidence supporting your ideas and providing a mineable data set. Coding interviews in this way surfaces patterns and themes and helps synthesize your thoughts, bridging the gap between qualitative and quantitative data by making it evident how many people share the same perspectives across interviews, thus adding extra weight to your recommendations.

COMPLETE THE INTERVIEWS WITHIN A FOCUSED TIMEFRAME

It's to your advantage to complete all the interviews within a concentrated three-to-four-week period. Without this kind of focus, you might forget sparks of insight and miss the coalescence of thought that flows from a concentrated collection of insights. Scheduling interviews can be the biggest challenge in making this happen. An automated calendar scheduling tool, like Calendly, can help smooth the scheduling process.

SEE WHAT THEY'RE SAYING

Of course, conducting interviews in person is ideal; however, Zoom videoconferencing calls are often the second most effective way to hear and *see* what people say in their interviews. Phone calls come in a distant third when it comes to gathering rich and productive insights. Seeing someone's facial expressions, hand gestures, and body language adds tremendous insight that informs your understanding of the *emotional significance* of their words.

INTERNAL INTERVIEWS

First, seek to understand your internal brand perspective by selecting executives and other leaders from across your company for an in-depth, one-on-one interview with you. Unless you have a particularly large or complex organization, completing interviews with five leaders of diverse perspectives is usually sufficient. This usually captures a representative internal view of how your company thinks customers and other external audiences perceive your brand compared to what they want those perceptions to be. Conducting all of the internal interviews on the same day adds clarity. When possible, scheduling the CEO for your last internal interview is a good practice because it creates a capstone dynamic—by the time you interview them, you'll understand the collective perspective of other company leaders and can use this final internal interview to resolve conflicting opinions or points of view and tie off any loose ends.

If your organization wants to include more voices in the Brand Discovery process than time-intensive in-depth interviews, transcriptions, and coding can accommodate, you can provide other leaders and employees with a questionnaire to cast a wider net, collect more data in support of your findings and recommendations, and enhance your ability to build buy-in by including more people. Of course, making an internal questionnaire available adds to your analysis workload, but it may be worth it depending on your company's political and cultural dynamic.

EXTERNAL INTERVIEWS

Curating a representative cross-section of customers (past, present, and future) along with partners and industry experts to interview is one of the best ways to build a brand that scales. There is no substitute for diving deep into how others perceive your brand. Doing so can unlock insights into why they think and feel the way they do about your brand and whether they think you can extend it in new directions. Many participants are willing to spend thirty to forty-five minutes doing an interview, though it can be challenging to schedule time with them if they're extremely busy. In those cases, it's essential for whoever has the best working relationship with them to extend the interview invitation to increase the likelihood of them accepting and keeping it.

Where appropriate, offering participants an honorarium can help motivate them to make and keep their interview appointments. The amount to offer varies by project and participant based on how much they value their time. Highly compensated professionals (doctors, dentists, attorneys, etc.) and executives may be accustomed to receiving hundreds of dollars for an hour or less of their time. In contrast, everyday consumers may be content with a thirty-dollar Amazon e-gift card.

Tripping Over the Truth

Strategic branding leaders and practitioners tune their antennae to recognize significant insights in the moment. The Brand Discovery process systematically prepares your mind to more fully identify, appreciate, capture, understand, and act on insights however subtle those signals might be. Without this heightened awareness, we may "trip over the truth" without realizing what we've stumbled upon.

While walking in the park with my wife one evening, I recognized the person approaching us as the opposing counsel from a difficult legal case I'd experienced. We were on a direct collision course, walking toward one another on a narrow paved path. When we passed one another, we simply said hello and kept walking. This close encounter with someone I'd only had limited interaction with under adverse circumstances initially flooded my mind with negative thoughts and emotions. But it also reframed my perception and helped me see this person as a human being; it reminded me that attorneys are people too—they go on walks and have lives beyond the courtroom. It reminded me of seeing my third-grade elementary school teacher shopping at the grocery store and realizing, perhaps for the first time, that she had a life outside the classroom.

This insight inspired me to write a successful slogan for a dental social media management company I was working with at the time: "Dentists Are People Too." Like attorneys, we sometimes forget that dentists are multidimensional people who have lives outside their professional interactions. They want patients to recognize, acknowledge, and appreciate them as real, relatable people with families, pursuits, and passions that extend beyond their sometimes-sterile office environments.

The insight behind this slogan reinforced the brand strategy of the business, which was to create relatable connections on social media between the real people behind the monolithic masks and white coats dentists wear and the patients they serve. The data showed the more engaged patients were with a doctor's social media pages, the more likely they were to remain loyal to their practice and refer friends and family to them.

To that end, T-shirts with our "Dentists Are People Too" slogan were so popular at industry events that fellow attendees, ranging from sixty-something dentists to twenty-something office managers, asked to take pictures with us wearing them throughout colossal convention halls at shows like the Greater New York Dental Meeting and show-cased them on their podcasts at the annual Healthcare Information and Management Systems Society (HIMSS) meeting. Other exhibitors and attendees *stole* them from our trade show booth, leaving in exchange their shirts tagged with sticky notes and scribbled apologies: "Hope you don't mind, but I had to have your shirt!" The reason for the resonance was an insight into an acute pain point dentists have—wanting patients to like them and relate to them as the caring, compassionate people they are, not just purveyors of pain.

Surface Significant, Actionable Insights

Unlike quantitative surveys, qualitative in-depth interviews are typically not trying to achieve statistical significance by converging on the best option from a predetermined set of choices. Instead, in-depth interviews generate new ideas that inform and inspire effective brand strategies, comprehensive messaging frameworks, compelling brand narratives, and engaging, creative campaigns.

Significant insights unlock new ways of thinking about your brand, business, or category. For example, in working with the city of Payson, Utah, we discovered an opportunity to reposition the community from being the home of onions—a default perception allowed to linger following a short-lived statewide agricultural initiative in the 1960s—to a new tagline and strategic intent: "Home to Adventure." The insights that led to this new direction came from observations and conversations with community leaders and residents about their love of the outdoors—not to mention Payson's recreation-friendly setting at the base of Mount Nebo with easy access to trail systems, streams, and sand dunes.

Exploring Payson's neighborhoods, we saw dozens of fifth-wheel trailers, campers, ATVs, side-by-sides, and dirt bikes. In-depth interviews highlighted a love of hiking, camping, fishing, mountain biking, road biking, and motorcycle riding among its citizens. In addition, annual community gatherings have formed generational ties for Payson's families and their posterity. The city serves over five thousand people at its annual salmon supper, which grew out of a church social. Its Scottish Festival celebrates the heritage of the city's founding families with tribal feats of strength, favorite foods, and bellowing bagpipes. The city hosts an annual parade and carnival, plus a weekly concert-in-the-park series during the summer on Sunday evenings. Adventure has always felt at home in Payson, but it wasn't until we took the time to uncover these insights and activate them that the city claimed its birthright and differentiated itself in the process.

By focusing on its new brand narrative, Payson is making it more attractive for like-minded residents, businesses, and organizations to call the city home, including an e-commerce company that fulfills millions of orders each year for dirt bike, ATV, UTV, ADV/dual sport, and e-bike equipment and gear; a technical skills community college; and an RV dealership.

Strategic, actionable insights have the potential to reframe your brand narrative, connect with new customers, and strengthen relationships with existing ones by creating a greater appreciation of the value your brand brings to their lives. Of course, you can test messaging and brand narratives in a statistically significant way if you have the time and money to do so, and we will address how to do that in a later chapter.

As you make a more deliberate effort to notice insights, honing your powers of perception and observation, you'll be surprised at how often you recognize them in daily life and how much more natural it will be to weave them into your work.

CHAPTER 3

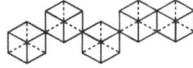

BRAND AUDIT

*"What makes his world so hard to see clearly
is not its strangeness but its usualness.
Familiarity can blind you, too."*

—Robert M. Pirsig

Familiarity can blind us to the changes we must make for our brands to be great. Whether it's an outdated value proposition failing to consider the new competitive reality, a physical space needing to be refreshed, a campaign that's no longer relevant, or a website that sounds and looks dated, giving yourself permission to call your own baby ugly can be hard to do. Even so, it's exactly what might be needed to build a brand that scales. You've got to retain your beginner's eyes and remain curious about how others see it. We've got to balance our branding priorities with empathy and appreciation for our customers and partners so our brands don't become self-serving.

Following our four-step process for conducting brand audits— gather, score, evaluate, and plan—can help. Please note the brand audit process applies to brand refresh and rebrand projects. You can skip this step altogether if you're creating a new brand.

The word "audit" can sound a little heavy, but conducting a well-rounded brand audit can help you reconsider what your brand stands for in context of the evolving market, ensuring your brand is still working as hard as it can for you. Think of it as a supportive 360-degree performance review with the intent of helping your brand get better.

Step 1: Gather

The first step in performing an effective brand audit is to gather representative examples of the brand touch points your organization currently creates, delivers, and facilitates for internal and external audiences. Brand touch points include the words, images, and experiences contributing to the perceptions—intentional or not—that internal and external audiences have of your brand. Some of the more apparent examples of touch points include your market-facing website, social media posts, sales presentations, advertising, and marketing collateral, along with email signatures, business cards, interior signage and design, swag, and trade show booth graphics.

Remember that everything communicates. Your office may look great and have an impressive lobby, but long hold times or an overflowing trash can in one of your restrooms can contradict and undermine those positive first impressions—as can colleagues working remotely whose cats nonchalantly walk in front of their screens on Zoom calls. Any incongruities can create "yes, but" moments, tilting the perception scale toward the negative. Back in the day, Fallon Worldwide, the award-winning ad agency headquartered in Minneapolis, staffed a bank of phones with professional receptionists who picked up the phone within one ring in contrast to the infamous and pervasive "Your call is important to us" voicemail message. Callers knew the agency valued them without having to be told. The more aware we are of what we're communicating—with or without words—the more aligned and effective we can be in creating and influencing our desired brand perceptions. The messages you want to convey through your touch points should be specific and unique to your business and the values of the people you serve.

A real estate brokerage we've worked with commissions paintings of their clients' family homes when the time comes for aging homeowners to sell them and move into an assisted living facility. This thoughtful memento shows their clients how much they care without having to say it. The partners of a professional services firm we've worked with invite new associates over for dinner at their homes to get to know them outside of the office. These dinners build personal relationships that strengthen ties to senior leadership and the firm to weather the inevitable ups and downs of work life.

Be resourceful. Designing thoughtful touch points doesn't have to cost a lot of time or money. Charlie Trotter, the celebrated chef in Chicago who pioneered farm-to-table practices in the late 1980s and early 1990s, along with producing award-winning cooking shows, gourmet products, cookbooks, and educational community outreach programs, purposefully asked his employees to park a few blocks away from his restaurant so they could pick up trash and cigarette butts off the ground as they walked the rest of the way to work.

Trotter also tore out the sidewalk and planted trees in the dark of night in front of his restaurant—without the city's permission—to beautify its curb appeal and enhance the overall aesthetic experience of dining there. Trotter drew inspiration from a threefold mission to make an aesthetic, cultural, and social contribution to the city and communities he and his business served, which informed all his branding decisions. A deep-rooted and ongoing commitment to upholding the highest standards of excellence was the organizing principle around which his multifaceted brand ecosystem revolved.

Be inclusive. Remember to consider what's important to *all* your audiences. Of course, your internal audiences will include your employees, executives, and shareholders, but it's also essential to include friends and family members—even employees' parents—depending on the culture. Howard Schultz gained a newfound appreciation of this internal-external branding principle when Starbucks entered the China market and discovered the company was interviewing not only prospective employees but also their parents—and that the people in China were interviewing the company and its leaders as much as or more than the other way around. In response, Starbucks held getting-to-know-you events where the employees' parents could get to know the company better and get behind the idea of their children working there. The decision carried added weight given the country's one-child policy at the time.[1]

In addition to typical external audiences like customers, former customers, prospective customers, and partners, consider what you're communicating (or not) to former employees. Look for untapped opportunities for connecting with, strengthening, and leveraging relationships with your alumni. After completing graduate school, my alma mater unceremoniously shut off my school-hosted email address. Instead, they could have allowed me to keep my school-issued email as an ongoing communication channel and invited me to transition to a new phase of our relationship to keep the conversation going. They could have seamlessly cultivated a lasting connection with me as a contributing member of their alumni community and a potential donor as my career progressed.

Be sure to include representatives from across departments throughout your organization to gather representative touch point examples and consider the messages these touch points communicate to your audiences. Pay special attention to all the ways in which your logo has been applied to different communication pieces and materials. The simple act of gathering all these examples can bring inconsistencies to light that may have previously gone unnoticed, including the incorrect use of your logos across departments and teams. Branding is certainly bigger than logos, but consistent visual communication is a cornerstone of effective brand communications. Use your brand audit to clarify and align everyone's use of your brand verbally, visually, and experientially for brand clarity and consistency.

Be objective. Consider conducting an objective baseline brand perception survey among customers and partners to determine how they broadly perceive your brand. You can periodically update your brand perception data to determine if the changes you've implemented are having the desired effect and adjust as needed. An annual study may provide the frequency needed to keep your finger on the pulse of how your brand is perceived in comparison to your desired perception. Your brand perception refresh rate will depend on how often you change your offerings as well as how frequently your competition changes their offerings and go-to-market strategies.

Working with a third-party survey provider can reinforce your strategic branding goals by ensuring your ongoing studies provide accurate data and a regular reporting cadence. Including a cross-section of executives and departments in the sponsorship and development of the survey will help increase the likelihood of getting their buy-in on the results and an ongoing commitment to investing resources in developing and implementing needed changes. Improving brand perception results will require everyone's best efforts, given the variety of disciplines involved in creating and delivering effective and consistent brand touch points companywide.

A well-designed brand perception study can give leaders the confidence to invest in new product development. It can help identify value propositions or benefits that resonate with customers and create buy-in from everyone in the company. After all, everyone must work together to live up to your brand promises, driving more revenue, profitability, loyalty, and advocacy. Cross-team collaboration is much easier to build and sustain when everyone is on board with brand-building goals and guidelines.

Step 2: Score

Once you've collected a well-rounded cross-section of brand touch point inputs, weigh and sort them based on their perceived value to your audiences and compare the relative importance of your audiences to one another. Conducting internal and external customer interviews and surveys can help inform this process—specifically, which touch points matter most to your most important audiences and *why*.

Audience scoring and ranking inputs and metrics will vary by industry. For SaaS companies, they include churn, customer acquisition cost (CAC), monthly recurring revenue (MRR), and customer lifetime value (CLV),[2] along with how much time and effort it takes to onboard, progress, maintain, and sustain those customer relationships from a customer or client success perspective. Businesses that sell clothing and other consumer goods directly to customers may place a premium on recency, frequency, and total monetary spend. Knowing what touch points matter most to your customers will help you design experiences that support those key interactions and create lasting relationships.

In addition to showcasing what features of a product or service matter most to specific customer segments, conjoint analysis can also help inform which customer touch points to focus on. The most crucial step in conducting any research is making sure the inputs inform the model and the analysis is done correctly so the outputs and recommendations truly represent what customers want.

When a brand has a clearly defined strategy, visual identity, and messaging framework, the gaps between its current and desired perceptions—and the touch points that reinforce or detract from them—become readily apparent. Organizing these gaps into one of three specific buckets helps make them clear and actionable at an overarching brand level or to a specific audience. The ideas and insights you gather will then inform the words, images, and experiences to define your future brand strategy.

Bucket 1: Visual gaps. The correct and consistent use of your visual brand identity is easy to see across various brand touch points. A thorough review will surface any discrepancies. Of course, you must first have visual brand standards to compare touch points against for this analysis to be worthwhile. These standards often take the form of a visual style guide, not to be mistaken with a brand book, which we'll discuss later. A visual style guide outlines the rules for correctly using your brand's logo, colors, typography, and other visual elements to create a cohesive look and feel for your brand. As your business grows and you begin to take your brand to market at scale, inconsistencies are more likely to happen as more individuals, teams, and agencies communicate on your behalf. All the more reason to establish visual brand standards before you scale and refresh them as needed.

If you're thinking about doing a brand refresh or complete rebrand, conducting a visual brand audit is less about comparing your existing visual brand communications to a set standard and more about learning what your current visual brand identity is and then communicating and understanding what it would take to change those perceptions if they're not on brand. Of course, you can skip this step for new brands.

Bucket 2: Verbal gaps. Defining guidelines for your brand voice and tone is another important aspect of shaping and influencing your desired brand perceptions. The publicly available Mailchimp Content Style Guide is a good example of a comprehensive set of brand voice guidelines.[3] It establishes clear parameters for communicating on behalf of Mailchimp with dos and don'ts for brand tone and voice and different types of communications and audiences. Though most companies' brand voice guidelines aren't as extensive, Mailchimp remains a good example to reference.

Depending on the number of offerings and audiences you have, you may want to consider creating different brand voice guidelines for different audiences. For example, marketing and selling to small- and medium-sized businesses differs from marketing and selling to enterprise customers. The vocabulary and degree of formality may need to change depending on your customer personas and the perceived value and risk associated with your products or services for each.

Bucket 3: Experiential gaps. The experiences customers have with your products and people significantly impact how they perceive your business and brand. It can be as simple as having plenty of grocery store staff members out on the floor and teaching them to walk a customer to where the orzo pasta sits on the shelf rather than waiting until the customer is checking out and asking, "Did you find everything okay?" with other people impatiently waiting behind them in line.

Customer service conversations can inform your experiential

discovery and reveal patterns of missed opportunities to satisfy, surprise, and delight them. If you're not a consumer of your own products and services, it's even more important to actively seek feedback from customers to learn how to help them feel the way you want them to about your business and brand.

Creating an intentional company culture is essential to living up to your brand promise at scale and building brand loyalty and advocacy. Clarifying your values and cultivating the beliefs and behaviors that bring them to life is core to creating experiences that keep customers and clients coming back for more (as we discuss in chapter 5). Experiential research can inform your current company culture and provide ways to improve it going forward.

Step 3: Evaluate

Deciding how much emphasis to give the gaps between your current and desired touch points can help you develop a plan to prioritize the right branding elements. Once you've collected examples of your current brand touch points, evaluate the degree to which they add to or subtract from how you want audiences to perceive your brand. Next, rank their relative importance to your customers and other audiences. Evaluation methods include customer surveys, in-person or by-phone interviews, and videoconference calls. Some brand touch points and audience segments carry more weight and importance than others. Factor the relative importance of each of your customer segments into your brand analysis. It's crucial to recognize it will take time and resources to address your brand gaps. These findings will help you make a case for securing support and resources to execute your plan.

Moreover, reviewing what you've learned from your brand audit as a collective team will help your organization realize branding is a shared responsibility reaching beyond the confines of individuals and teams with "brand" or "marketing" in their titles. Branding is ultimately everyone's responsibility because creating and delivering compelling brand images, messages, and experiences crosses departmental lines. The goal of a well-crafted brand strategy is to inspire and guide leaders to organize their teams and make it happen.

Some branding objectives remain constant while others change or become irrelevant. For example, establishing and maintaining your brand as the category leader will likely be an ongoing priority, whereas conducting a successful product launch or seasonal campaign will be a short-term focus. Before conducting a study, be sure to clearly define meaningful objectives and metrics. Include questions that invite customers to share their ideas on where they think your brand can go from here. Extending a brand can be tricky, so consulting with your customers on future growth before committing resources can help you make wise investments.

Step 4: Plan

Take time to review the findings of your brand evaluation and extract general guiding principles from them for your brand strategy. While it's helpful to list incongruencies and inconsistencies at a touch point level, it's even more important to highlight major themes and use them to set the strategic direction for your brand. Rather than getting bogged down in the details, summarize actionable, high-level brand takeaways and enlist the help of the right individuals and teams to take your brand where you want it to go. We've found it helpful to summarize these takeaways in imperative sentences, briefly describing what should be done differently in the future.

CHAPTER 4

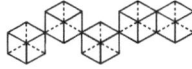

COMPETITIVE ANALYSIS

"In 1945, the world was in a shambles. American companies had no competition. So, nobody really thought much about quality. Why should they? The world bought everything America produced. It was a prescription for disaster."

—W. Edwards Deming

Competition can bring out the best in us when we are committed to winning the hearts and minds of our customers. Rather than being intimidated or discouraged, Michelangelo drew inspiration from the twisting torsos of other artists' works to level up his game and accomplish similar feats of artistry in his sculptures. As a result, he took his work to an entirely new level of realistic humanism and anatomical accuracy. We can use competitors' gains as fuel to improve our performance too.

When the competition makes a discovery or masters a technique we lack, we can use their advantage as inspiration and motivation to master skills and rival or exceed their performance. If we get complacent and take our success for granted, we may be upended by a new competitor that blows by us because we're on cruise control.

Objectively viewing customers' current perceptions of your brand in view of the competitive landscape will help you make informed decisions about where to take your brand next. Typically, the mental map customers have of your category has room for two brands that can solve their problem. Think Spotify and Pandora, Apple and Microsoft, or Hertz and Avis. Sure, there are many more providers in most markets, and we may use some of them occasionally, but as customers with short attention spans, we tend to reduce any market down to the two biggest competitors to minimize complexity. Learning how customers see the competition relative to the problem you solve is critical to positioning your brand as the category leader.

Substitutes and Alternatives

In scanning the competitive landscape, it's not difficult to identify direct competitors vying for the same customers through the same channels and similar business models. How often have we seen a Burger King restaurant sitting kitty-corner from a McDonald's restaurant at the same intersection? Identifying indirect competitors, however, is often more enlightening and advantageous.

The authors of the acclaimed business book *Blue Ocean Strategy* explain that "substitutes have the same form but different functions: Model T car vs. horse-drawn carriage for transportation. Alternatives have different forms and functions, but the same purpose: eating dinner at a restaurant vs. going to the movies to enjoy a night out."[1] Zooming out on your competitive context to consider substitutes and alternatives provides added insight into what your customers are doing to satisfy their unmet needs and, in turn, helps inform and refine your response. Remember to see the competitive landscape through the eyes of your customers so you don't miss indirect competitors that may be diverting customers away from you.

As Harvard Business School professor Clayton Christensen taught, the competitive context for your product or service includes any "jobs" customers are currently "hiring" to do that your product could satisfy for them. Christensen's "jobs to be done" framework gives us another way to view the competition in light of entirely new sets of substitutes and alternatives we might have overlooked. When consulting with a national restaurant chain, Christensen observed that while some customers hired milkshakes as a treat for themselves or their kids, others hired them to make their morning commutes more exciting and fun. These new insights gave the restaurant new ideas for product development, including marketing milkshakes and other products as a way to make morning commutes more satisfying and interesting for customers.

The same types of inputs for your brand audit apply to analyzing your competition, including the words, images, and experiences your competitors use to try and differentiate and communicate their value to give customers credible reasons to choose them.

Customer Input

Remember to include your customers in choosing the companies and brands to incorporate in your analysis. Ultimately, your customers decide what your brand is in context of the competitive landscape. Consult your customers regarding who they see as your main competition and ask them why those competitors win against you—and vice versa—as far as that customer is concerned. Talking to several customers from each of your market segments will help you see the competition through their eyes.

The customers of the Cricut creative enablement tool I mentioned earlier saw it as a replacement for their mothers' Singer sewing machines. The two tools were entirely different, but they overlapped in giving customers a creative outlet and receiving appreciative compliments from others in response to their work. Interestingly, no one from the client company talked about this connection of the Cricut being a creative outlet like the sewing machine was for the previous generation. This insight came to light only after conducting a series of interviews with customers from across the country. After three to five people mentioned it, we knew we were onto something. We realized the client company had struck a chord with customers who deeply resonated with their brand at a fundamental level because, without it, they would not have had an outlet for their hidden creative talent.

Pattern Recognition

One of the most essential skills to develop in competitive analysis is the ability to see and recognize patterns. Finding these patterns requires multiple data points and inputs, so it helps to reach beyond the tendency to focus on one or two competitors. Including at least three to five competitors in your analysis is essential, as well as the consideration of substitutes and alternatives. And you must read between the lines in the data.

An industrial company we worked with had a very product-centric website. It looked and felt like a "speeds and feeds" product catalog with lots of features but very few benefits or outcomes and no pictures of the people using their products. Having completed their customer interviews, we knew how interesting and colorful the people who use their products are. Our client's competitors' websites focused on their products and product features as well. The few pictures of people were contrived and unrealistic.

As a result of seeing how similar these websites were to one another, we saw an opportunity for our client to make the customer the hero of their story by showing photos and videos of real customers out in the field using their products. This insight inspired differentiated ideas for their brand purpose, position, promise, pillars, and personality.

Connecting the Dots

In his masterpiece, *Un dimanche après-midi à l'Île de la Grande Jatte* (*A Sunday on La Grande Jatte*), painter Georges Seurat used pointillism, "a highly systematic and scientific technique based on the hypothesis that closely positioned points of pure color mix together in the viewer's eye."[2] The effect creates a luminous illusion best viewed at a distance as the dots of color merge and form the image.

Similarly, the dot-to-dot collection of competitive analysis data inputs is best viewed at a distance by the brand strategist to see the picture they form as a whole. Ideally, competitive analysis work is done over a period of time that allows for breaks between working sessions so new insights and ideas can coalesce and cure as you reflect on your ideas from previous sessions and build on and refine your initial findings.

Reframing the Picture

The way we frame what we learn from a thorough and thoughtful analysis of the competitive field is equally important to the content of the analysis. The Art Institute of Chicago went to great lengths to re-create the plain white frame Georges Seurat specified for his masterwork, a departure from the gold frames popular in the late 1800s. Similarly, the way you frame the insights you gather from your competitive analysis ought to add to and enhance the competitive picture that informs your brand strategy.

The Sea of Sameness

When we facilitated VitalSmarts's rebrand to Crucial Learning, its chief marketing officer, Mary McChesney, commented on how similar everything looks at learning and development industry conferences and trade shows. Under Mary's leadership, the company took a different approach with its new visual brand identity and set itself apart by taking their look and feel in a different direction. The new approach was informed, in part, by how the other players in their space had assimilated into an implicit consensus around industry norms. When you see everyone doing similar things in similar ways, it's an opportunity to differentiate your brand by doing different things and doing things differently, which Paul Gustavson of Organization Planning and Design teaches his clients is the essence of strategy. Applying these principles to brand strategy means *doing different things* that create differentiated offerings that solve real customer problems, and it's foundational to creating perceived value in their minds and the marketplace. *Doing things differently* means that although you and your competitors may do some of the same things, finding ways to do them differently can help set your brand and business apart.

In *Playing to Win*, Roger Martin and A. G. Lafley discuss making a series or "cascade" of strategic questions and choices to guide the development of an effective and differentiated strategy. Martin and Lafley applied this process in guiding Procter & Gamble (P&G) to continued growth and success. Their five-part choice cascade includes answering the following questions:

1. **What is your winning aspiration?** To answer, you must know what you want to achieve as an organization and articulate it in a way that inspires and motivates your people.

2. **Where will you play?** The goal here is to identify the customers, consumers, markets, channels, product categories, vertical stages, and stages of industries that give you the best chance of winning.

3. **How will you win in chosen markets?** This step in strategy development helps sharpen how you will win within your chosen field of competition. It goes hand in hand with the where-to-play choice.

4. **What capabilities must be in place to win?** Pinpoint the specific capabilities and competencies that will give your brand a competitive edge.

5. **What management systems are required?** Define and map out the systems and measures to support your strategy.[3]

Lafley and Martin remind us that creating an effective and differentiated strategy is an iterative, nonlinear process. Having a clear understanding of the competition and how it answers these questions is critical to strategy development. Brand strategy informs business strategy and vice versa. Think of it as a double-helix DNA-like dynamic where one strand of information and insight feeds the other. The more differentiated the answers to these five questions, the harder it will be for competitors to replicate your success. The more differences between you and your competition, the more clearly customers can discern your value as being different from alternatives and substitutes and the more difficult it can be for competitors to copy you.

Bringing It All Together

Brand strategy blends these elements by combining insights about the company, its customers, competition, and creativity into one cohesive direction. An unlikely but good illustration of this blending process in action is the work we've done branding cities, towns, and counties in our home market here in Utah. The state's most populous areas are along the base of the Wasatch Mountains, and because of their shared geographical setting, many leaders of these communities landed on one of two elements: (1) a landmark building or (2) an image of the mountains with a rising sun coming up behind them.

When cities, towns, and counties rely on these obvious and undifferentiated features, the result is a series of lookalike logos that aren't differentiating and don't create a distinctive brand identity. In contrast, we believe each city and community has something unique about its culture and values that sets it apart. The insights needed to define differentiated brand strategies come from in-depth Brand Discovery and competitive analysis.

For the city of Mapleton, Utah, our Brand Discovery and competitive analysis worked to give it a unique and meaningful brand strategy that sets its slogan and visual brand identity apart in a way that is authentic to its founding families and their shared community values, even as dramatic development and growth continue with new people moving in by the dozens. Two significant insights drove Mapleton's brand strategy. First, the residents feel it's a small town, and second, they believe in serving and helping one another.

Even though our competitive analysis showed Mapleton has technically outgrown the formal definition of what it means to be a "town," residents still *feel* like it's a small town and want to hold on to that feeling despite its tremendous growth. An eighty-nine-year-old Caucasian man born and raised in Mapleton said, "I've always felt that there was a special spirit in Mapleton that may be different from some other places: more supportive, more friendly. The spirit of good neighbors and respecting each other. The feeling of security and belonging relieves some worries. The fear of being alone and the challenges that the world has for us. Just knowing that if you need help, you've got it."

A twenty-something African American man affirmed these sentiments, saying, "The Mapleton community is somehow big and small all at the same time. It's a big, small town, which is really fun . . . . My brother had a rare form of cancer while he was in Mapleton, and our immediate neighbors rallied around him. That doesn't happen in other communities. When one of us is down, everybody is down and affected. There's just a general love and care that all the residents have for each other."

Insights like these were confirmed throughout the Brand Discovery process. At our recommendation, the city of Mapleton adopted a new slogan we developed for them: "Small Town. Big Heart." We brought this notion to life visually using a logo inspired by a community barn raising that was part of Mapleton's cherished history. Residents of the city have commented on how well the city's new slogan and identity reflect how they feel about their town; some get emotional just talking about it. They love the new logo and what it represents. No other city in Utah has a slogan or logo like Mapleton's. That's the goal of branding—to set your brand apart and create your desired brand perception.

Of course, Mapleton will have to make its slogan and logo matter by creating memorable experiences for its residents and visitors, which it continues to do.

Different and Relevant

Simply being different is not good branding. Your brand has got to be both different and relevant; it has to matter to the right people and make the right impression. If your brand strategy leads to a branding direction that is different but irrelevant or off-putting to your intended audiences, then it has failed. Knowing what is relevant comes from the in-depth interview process, while the competitive analysis process informs what is different. Both elements are necessary for creating a winning brand strategy.

From/To Statements

Consolidating all these insights and elements into a succinct summary of brand takeaways is very helpful. One of the most effective ways to contrast your current brand with your desired future state is to create a list of From/To statements based on what you've learned. On the left side is a list of how your brand is perceived today, and on the right side is a list of how you want your brand to be in the future. This simple synopsis creates clarity and starts mapping a path forward and building agreement around future branding initiatives.

Remember to stay relatively high level in creating your From/To summary. You want people on your team to understand the strategic direction the brand needs to take without getting tangled up in the details or trying to outline all the tactical steps required to bring about those results. There will be plenty of opportunities to reach into the specifics. First and foremost, you've got to build buy-in for your new brand strategy.

Competitive analysis is an essential ingredient in creating an effective brand strategy. It helps you gain a more objective understanding of whether or not your offering is truly differentiated. Knowing who your competitors are and how you win against them from a customer perspective puts you in a position of strength because it shows you how they view the market. It gives you a mental map of where they see you playing and how they see you winning. It requires humility because you may not like what you hear, but it can inspire you to make the necessary changes to be more relevant to your customers.

PHASE 2

BRAND FOUNDATION

*"You can't build a great building on a weak foundation.
You must have a solid foundation if you're
going to have a strong superstructure."*

—Gordon B. Hinckley

During college, I had a summer job working on a footing and foundation crew for new ski resort accommodations and high-end homes in Park City, Utah. My responsibilities included carrying forms from our truck to the holes dug for the building foundations. In addition to carrying the forms, I sprayed them with oil so the cement wouldn't stick to them when it had dried, something like cooking spray on a muffin tin.

I also tied reinforcing steel with wire that held the rebar in place until we poured concrete into the forms, where it would harden and form a sure foundation that would withstand extreme weather conditions for years. The structures we built included retaining walls that held back dirt from the sides of the mountains where we worked. We built walls up to thirty feet tall, supported by scaffolding and small wedged metal plates that kept the forms in place while we set them up. Everyone on our crew was mindful of the exposed rebar below us as we worked on the walls; our high-wire guys tethered themselves to the scaffolding with safety harnesses to ensure they didn't fall.

The walls we built had to be plumb, level, and square to support the luxury hotel that would be built upon them after our part of the project was finished. Plumb ensures a foundation is true to the vertical plane, level ensures it's true to the horizontal plane, and square ensures that when a plumb object intersects with a level object, they form a ninety-degree angle. Anything less than meeting these standards would make a foundation vulnerable to failure under pressure.

When the cement trucks arrived at a jobsite, they extended long hoses called booms to funnel the cement where it needed to go, reaching out over the foundation. Experienced crew members climbed to the top of the narrow walls to direct the boom and fill the forms with concrete. It was hot, heavy work, but it was satisfying to see the finished result when we peeled the forms off the walls, carried them back to the truck, and moved on to our next project. Without a strong foundation, these buildings would have collapsed and sloughed off the mountain during the winter runoff in the spring when the freezing snow passed the baton to the burning sun.

Like the firm foundation of a building, your Brand Foundation helps ensure the strength and structural integrity of your brand for years to come. The elements of your Brand Foundation are relatively timeless, providing continuity that surpasses changing leadership and sustains alignment that informs your brand strategy and implementation across your team.

Ideally, your brand purpose ought to be evergreen, remaining constant for all time. You may need to adjust your brand position periodically to reflect new offerings from your business or in response to competitive pressures. You may also need to periodically review your brand promise to see if adjustments are required when you bring new products, services, or solutions to market so you're not leaving any money on the table in how you communicate the overarching value you deliver to customers. You may need to update your brand pillars from time to time as you innovate new differentiators. However, your brand personality rarely changes.

The insights you uncover in Phase 1, Brand Discovery, are the reinforcing steel within Phase 2, when you form and pour your brand's concrete footings and foundation. The two phases work together, making sure your Brand Foundation is plumb, level, and square, giving it the rigor it needs to support the pressure of the brand building on top of it and ensuring its ability to withstand rough winds and weather from the competing interests within and without your organization.

It takes patience to see Phases 1 and 2 through to completion because this work is mainly belowground. For the first few months, you may not see anything but a big hole with piles of dirt beside it on your jobsite. Individuals who are unfamiliar with or indirectly involved in the branding process may wonder if anything's getting done; they'll want to know when they can expect to see the results from your organization's investment in time and resources. Digging deep into your brand soil to understand what it's made of and ensure it's stable, forming your foundation, and tying reinforcing insights into it from Phase 1 requires sustained focus, effort, and time. You can't cut corners without compromising the long-term viability and staying power of your brand.

Once your Brand Foundation is secure, you can confidently build your Brand Expression on top of it, including your messaging framework, brand narrative, brand architecture, and visual brand identity—along with all the brand performance revenue-generation activities in Phase 4, Brand Activation. A strong Brand Foundation helps you build your brand in a way that is aligned and congruent with your brand strategy to reinforce your desired brand perception. Each of the five elements within Phase 2, Brand Foundation, builds on the last to create a structurally sound foundation.

CHAPTER 5

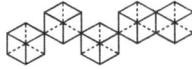

BRAND PURPOSE

*"What you do makes a difference, and you have to decide
what kind of difference you want to make."*

—Jane Goodall

When Simon Sinek gave his TEDxPugetSound talk on the Golden Circle, he lit a fire in people that still burns brightly today. With more than sixty million views at the time of this printing, Sinek has shown the world once again that an idea can change hearts and minds and create a movement. With his simple, insightful framework, he popularized the idea of building a purpose-driven organization and creating brand stories that *Start with Why*, the title of his first best-selling book.

His framework revolves around insights into how the human mind works, starting with *why* people do what they do, then *how* they do what they do, followed by *what* they do.[1] Though many organizations tell their stories in the opposite direction—what, how, why—Sinek says when you start with why and work your way out through how and what, you connect with people on a values-based and emotional level. If you buy Sinek's argument, the question then becomes: How do you create and write an effective purpose statement and get your organization to embrace it?

Start with Why came out in 2009, the same year Roy Spence, the adman who built the advertising agency GSD&M, which developed successful brands for Southwest Airlines, Walmart, DreamWorks, the PGA Tour, the United States Air Force, and the Texas Department of Transportation (TxDOT) among others, published *It's Not What You Sell, It's What You Stand For: Why Every Extraordinary Business Is Driven by Purpose*. Both books make a case for building purpose-driven organizations, though, in my opinion, Roy Spence does a better job of explaining how to write an effective purpose statement.

In his book, Spence says Jim Collins and Jerry Porras, the authors of *Built to Last* (1994), got it right when they defined a purpose statement as follows:

> CORE PURPOSE is the organization's fundamental reason for being. An effective purpose reflects the importance people attach to the company's work—it taps their idealistic motivations—and gets at reasons for an organization's existence beyond making money.[2]

PURPOSE STATEMENTS WE'VE WRITTEN

Bacon (temp work app for the gig economy):

"To show the world what a little hustle can do"

Spence explains, "Purpose is a definitive statement about the difference you are trying to make in the world."[3] And he should know, having penned organization-defining purpose statements like "To give people the freedom to fly" for Southwest Airlines and "To save people money so they can live better" for Walmart. Examples of purpose statements from other companies include the following:

Nike: "To provide innovation and inspiration for every athlete in the world. (And if you have a body, you're an athlete.)"

Target: "To help all families discover the joy of everyday life."

Tesla: "To accelerate the world's transition to sustainable energy."

Notice how concise these purpose statements are and how they allude to both the business of these brands and the audiences they serve without overtly mentioning how and what they do. This is an essential aspect of well-crafted purpose statements, especially considering that the how and what for these businesses will most likely change in time, whereas their purposes won't.

Spence further clarifies these reasons why you should want a purpose statement for your organization:

Purpose drives everything. It will drive all major decision-making and become the determining factor in how you allocate resources, hire employees, plan for the future, and judge your success. Purpose is a path to high performance. It fulfills people's deep-seated needs and will drive preference for your company.

Purpose fosters visionary ideas and meaningful innovation. It provides the motivation and direction necessary to create meaningful innovation.

Purpose moves mountains. It can rally the troops to overcome seemingly insurmountable odds.

Purpose will hold you steady in a turbulent marketplace. It will see you through when times get tough and the road seems unclear.

Purpose injects your brand with a healthy dose of reality. It's not something you can fake. It's genuine. It's real. It's something your customers honestly appreciate about you.

Purpose recruits passionate people. It will make your organization more attractive to value-based, passionate people.

Purpose brings energy and vitality to the work at hand. It provides meaningful and sustainable motivation for employees.

Purpose contributes to a life well lived. Work is no longer about a 9-to-5 job to be endured but a meaningful source of fulfillment and satisfaction.[4]

At Backstory, we've found all these reasons for wanting a purpose statement to be true. My wife and I walked through our new neighborhood one Sunday afternoon and talked with a couple in their front yard. Their twenty-something daughter had just come out of their house and joined our conversation when they asked me what I did for a living. I explained Backstory builds brands that live up to their promise and that, among other companies, we'd worked with BambooHR, a popular SaaS company in the HR space that happens to be headquartered in our area.

At this point in the conversation, the daughter of our new friends lit up and spontaneously said, "I love BambooHR!" When I asked her why, she said, "I just started working there, and I love their purpose." When I asked her what BambooHR's purpose was, she spontaneously and enthusiastically answered saying, "We set people free to do great work!"

She didn't have to look at a cheat sheet. No one was handing out twenty-dollar bills to any employee who could recite the purpose statement correctly at an all-hands meeting. She shared her employer's purpose without hesitation because she'd internalized it. She'd bought into it because she identified with what the words said, and, more importantly, she bought into what it feels like to work at BambooHR, which was wholly and entirely consistent with their purpose statement.

It was gratifying to know that even though she'd just started working at BambooHR a few months prior, the company's purpose statement resonated deeply with this recent college graduate. She didn't know I'd helped the company articulate its purpose eight years earlier. Seeing this intelligent, talented young woman share her company's purpose statement with us in such an impromptu way so many years after it was written started me thinking about the power of keeping purpose statements simple. As tempting as it can be to try and say too much, the power of well-crafted purpose statements is their simplicity.

PURPOSE STATEMENTS WE'VE WRITTEN

Grow (no-code, full-stack business intelligence SaaS):

"To empower everyone to make data-driven decision

Another time, Saul Leal, the founder and CEO of OneMeta, a client of ours in the AI translation and transcription industry, was meeting with a group of leaders and prospective customers from the education industry when one of them asked him what his purpose was. At first, Saul started describing his technology and products (his company's how and what), but the customer persisted in asking about his purpose. That's when Saul remembered to share the purpose we'd developed with him, "To create a more understanding world," as his why. After hearing it, the individual hugged him and sincerely said, "That's my purpose too!" Saul connected on a deeper and more personal level by finding common, transcendent ground with this prospective customer rather than simply talking about features and benefits.

A third example is from a financial services company, LJ Cooper, whose original founders left the company, leaving new clients wondering where LJ was. In the Brand Discovery process, we uncovered insights into the hearts and minds of the current core leadership team. They were sincerely committed to helping their clients do something purposeful with their money once they had more than enough to live comfortably through retirement.

These leaders shared stories about money-motivated clients who repeatedly moved the finish line on themselves when they reached a financial goal because it seemed one could never have enough of something that wasn't truly satisfying. Instead, the leaders of LJ Cooper found it much more effective to help clients identify what mattered most to them and work toward funding and fulfilling that purpose rather than just reaching an arbitrary number. One partner shared a story about convincing a client to purchase a wheelchair-accessible van for her ailing husband. She'd been nervous about drawing money from their retirement account, not wanting to erode their nest egg. He reassured her they would be okay and helped her make the purchase, giving her husband and herself newfound mobility. Another client talked about how much it meant to her that a partner at the firm amplified her vision for sponsoring a 5K fundraiser. With his help, she grew her idea into a full-length marathon with more support and participation than she'd thought possible. Inspiring stories like these pointed toward rebranding the firm as FirstPurpose Wealth to reflect its high-road commitment to helping clients find and fund their purpose.

PURPOSE STATEMENTS WE'VE WRITTEN

Kinect Capital [501(C)(3) nonprofit organization]:

"To make entrepreneurs more investable
and connect them to capital"

A memorable, motivating purpose statement needs to be authentic. There is no cookie-cutter template to create yours; it has to be true and genuine to your organizational and personal values. Here are a few guidelines to get you there.

Inspirational and motivational: A well-crafted purpose statement should inspire the company's leaders and team members, bringing out the best in them. That isn't to say everyone will find the same purpose statement equally inspiring and motivating. If a member of your team doesn't care about the audiences your brand serves, chances are they're not going to identify with your organization's purpose no matter how inspiring or motivating it is for you and your core team.

In reflecting on the significance of a clearly defined purpose for building BambooHR, cofounder Ryan Sanders said, "If your sole focus is on making money, it's not a motivating reason to get out of bed. Discovering your purpose carries substantial power. It becomes invaluable during the tough times businesses inevitably face, whether you're curled up on your living room floor, worried about meeting payroll, surviving a pandemic, or losing a key employee you believed would never depart. It serves as your guiding star."[5]

The aperture principle: In writing your purpose statement, remember to be specific enough to orient your internal and external audiences to where you play in your industry and category but not so specific as to box your business in and limit its growth potential. As with the f-stop settings of a camera lens, if your aperture is too narrow, your purpose will be unclear, underlit, and underdeveloped. On the other hand, if your aperture is too broad and your purpose statement is too high level, abstract, or far removed from what you do and who you serve, the image you create for your brand may be blurry, washed out, and overexposed. Too many purpose statements are too vague. For example, declaring your purpose is "To change the world" is far too broad to be meaningful.

Likewise, a purpose statement that is too niche can be so narrow it becomes inconsequential or too short-lived. Ideally, your purpose statement should represent such a big idea that you'll never fully accomplish it but be focused enough that you continually work toward it. Simon Sinek delves into this topic in detail in *The Infinite Game*.

Keeping it simple and keeping it real: In writing purpose statements, we've found a pattern I first saw at a Patagonia store in Hawaii helpful. Given its deeply purposeful approach to business, it's not surprising that Patagonia would put its purpose front and center in its stores. The sign simply read, "We're in business to save our home planet." While it's true the company makes outdoor gear and apparel (the what), the reason for the company's existence, its raison d'être (the why), is to save our home planet. The company's environmental activism is well known. Yvon Chouinard's commitment to his company's purpose is so sincere he essentially gave the company away in 2022, ensuring Patagonia's purpose would continue being the primary reason for its existence well beyond his own.

Room for more: Interestingly, purpose statements can make a difference for companies that compete in the same industries with similar hows and whats. Like Patagonia, Cotopaxi is a successful outdoor clothing and gear company but with a different purpose from Patagonia's that has helped inform and guide a different set of strategic choices. On a product level, one could argue that the two companies appear to overlap so much as to be interchangeable, but however similar and competitive their offerings may appear, their purposes speak to different people for different reasons.

"In the early years of Cotopaxi, a venture capital firm told me they wouldn't invest because they didn't believe we could compete against Patagonia," says Davis Smith, the founder of Cotopaxi. "Patagonia is a brand I've respected for years, and Cotopaxi's purpose is unique. Cotopaxi's mission extends beyond saving our planet (although 94 percent of our product is made of remnant, recycled, or responsible materials) and deeply focuses on saving humanity. Protecting our planet and fighting extreme poverty are inextricably linked; we can't save one without the other. I hope the future is full of Patagonias and Cotopaxis. . . . There could never be too many companies committed to changing capitalism for the better."[6] Even if another company does share a similar purpose statement to yours, the way you fulfill that purpose is what truly sets you apart.

PURPOSE STATEMENTS WE'VE WRITTEN

MPWR (door-to-door solar sales and marketing company):

"To set salespeople free"

Different means to the same end: You know you've found your purpose statement when you feel so committed to it that if your business went away, you would still be committed to finding another path to accomplish it because it aligns so strongly with your values. During the COVID-19 pandemic, Simon Sinek did an interview where he was asked if organizations should change their purpose if their current business models failed. True to his principles, Sinek answered by saying your how and what can pivot and change, but your why should remain the same, even during turbulent times.

In response to the pandemic, Sinek shifted the economic engine of his business model from giving $150,000 per-hour keynote speeches at corporate events and conferences to providing online courses, establishing a different way to live his organization's purpose, which is "To inspire people to do the things that inspire them so that, together, each of us can change our world for the better."[7] Once you've established a soulful purpose for your organization, it becomes your guiding North Star. It's always there, constantly guiding your path and decisions to align with your most deeply held beliefs and values.

Mission, Vision, and Values

We're often asked how purpose statements relate to mission, vision, and values statements. Here again, Roy Spence does a nice job of clarifying the relationship between purpose, mission, and vision statements. Simply stated, purpose statements articulate the difference you make beyond making money, the change you want to make in the world. Mission statements articulate *how* you make that difference. Your vision statement describes how you see the world as you fulfill your purpose.

MISSION

Building on the previous example from Southwest Airlines and its purpose—"To give people the freedom to fly"—its mission fulfills that purpose. "By keeping fares low and spirits high" is consistent with the company's fun-loving and hospitable culture. Whenever you see a purpose statement that includes the word "by," it signals the company has coupled its purpose and mission statements. Whatever follows the word "by" is the mission statement: it's how the company accomplishes its purpose, and it maps beautifully to the how in Simon Sinek's Golden Circle.

For example, the Walt Disney Company says, "We create happiness [that's the purpose statement] by providing the best in entertainment for people of all ages everywhere [that's the mission statement]." And by the way, your organization may have more than one mission, which you can easily include in the mission portion of your foundational brand story.

VISION

Spence defines Southwest's vision as the following: "We see a world where everyone can travel." Note that vision statements differ from BHAGs (big, hairy, audacious goals), also defined by Jim Collins and Jerry Porras in their book *Built to Last*. Whereas BHAGs are clear, compelling stretch goals, vision statements describe how the world will be when you have made significant progress toward fulfilling your purpose. Your vision isn't about your company, it's about the way you want the world to be.

VALUES

Core values define your company culture, the ideals, beliefs, and behaviors you live by to fulfill your purpose. Southwest cultivates a heartfelt people-first culture that starts with its employees and extends to its customers and partners.

BambooHR defines its culture this way:

- Assume the best.

- Be open.

- Do the right thing.

- Enjoy quality of life.

- Grow from good to great.

- Lead from where you are.

- Make it count.

These beliefs and behaviors are deeply rooted in the personal values of the founders of BambooHR and the kind of unique company culture they wanted to create. They didn't simply look at other companies' values and copy-paste them as their own. They took time to reflect on the attitudes and behaviors they wanted to define *their* company's cultural values.

PURPOSE STATEMENTS WE'VE WRITTEN

Nano-Yield (nanoliquid technology company):

"To deliver on the promise of nanotechnology
for all types of growers"

Clients often ask us whether their purpose, mission, vision, and values statements are meant to be market- or external-facing or reserved for internal use only. Purpose statements can be market-facing, though how you incorporate your purpose statement into your brand story can vary from leading with it by, for example, weaving it into the above-the-fold messaging of your home page or talking about it more subtly as part of your about us statement and other supporting elements of your story.

Vision and values statements tend to be more internal facing to guide and inform your team's decisions and behavior, but that doesn't mean they can't be accessible to the public. That said, more than merely reading your vision and values, your external audiences should *feel* their effects through your offerings and how you deliver them. BambooHR openly and readily shares its brand purpose with all its audiences on the "About" page of its market-facing website; more importantly, the company strives to live its brand purpose through its interactions with employees and customers every day, so they experience and feel it transmitted through thousands of touch points with BambooHR throughout years of positive interactions.

Who We Are Is More Important Than What We Do

As the founder and chairman of Quicken Loans, now Rocket Mortgage, Dan Gilbert built and scaled a hugely successful business and a personal net worth of more than $20 billion by carefully curating and teaching a culture of excellence "engineered to amaze" customers. What better way to differentiate your offering in a highly regulated industry where the Federal Reserve determines mortgage rates?

In his 2017 book, *ISMs in Action*, Gilbert shares nineteen culture-defining "ISMs," or beliefs and behaviors, that define the culture of Rocket Mortgage and his other Rocket Companies. Having attended one of his ISM days in Detroit, I was impressed that Gilbert didn't delegate the responsibility of teaching his culture to others. He was onstage, in person, all day, teaching the ISMs himself. When I asked him why, he said, "Bathing our employees in our culture is the best investment of my time because *who* we are is more important than *what* we do. Once you know who you are and choose to see the world through that prism, every decision that needs to be made and every action taken becomes a lot easier." His ISMs define the Rocket Mortgage philosophy and cultural DNA.

Gilbert and his team curated, collected, and wrote the ISMs from observations and lessons learned in building and scaling a business with over ten thousand employees. These behavioral guidelines include mantras like "Every client. Every time. No exceptions. No excuses." The way I heard Gilbert teach his people how to apply this guiding principle is that every Rocket Mortgage employee is expected to return every customer's voicemail and email within twenty-four hours. And Out of the Office (OOO) email subject lines aren't allowed at the company because Gilbert and his team are committed to ensuring that their customers' mortgage applications continue to progress even when coworkers take vacations, are out on maternity or paternity leave, or call in sick. Someone keeps your mortgage moving forward regardless.

Another ISM, "Always raising our level of awareness," encourages employees to let Gilbert know (via text or email) when something is below Rocket Mortgage's standards. When Gilbert or his team receives feedback from his army of awareness-raising team members that some aspect of the Rocket Mortgage experience is off brand, no matter how obscure, he has a team of people who fix and remedy these lapses and gaps that could detract from who Rocket Mortgage is at its best.

PURPOSE STATEMENTS WE'VE WRITTEN

Property Management Inc./PMI
(property management franchisor):
"To open doors to a better life"

For example, a Rocket Mortgage employee noticed a dumpster overflowing with trash near the company's parking garage. Although the business's online customers would never see it, that employee knew this situation was inconsistent with the high standards the company upholds, so they texted Gilbert, and the problem was resolved within twenty-four hours. Employees working in downtown Detroit at the company's headquarters observed the clock outside of a neighborhood bank was slow by ten minutes. They contacted the bank to let them know about the problem and asked them to fix it. When nothing happened, the Rocket Mortgage employees escalated it to Gilbert's attention. He called the bank president, and the time was right on the clock the next day. Rocket Mortgage didn't relent because allowing that clock to continue displaying the wrong time would reflect poorly on their business community.

Some may question the need and appropriateness of a mortgage company telling a bank to adjust its clock. But to Gilbert and his Rocket Mortgage employees, it made perfect sense because the bank's level of professionalism makes an impression on Rocket Mortgage's employees and customers by virtue of the fact that Rocket Mortgage purposefully set up its headquarters in downtown Detroit to help revitalize the city. The company's leaders know little things can make a big impression, and they want everyone in the business community to think well of Rocket Mortgage and deservedly so.

The company is serious about its employees living up to the performance standards set by the ISMs and expects employees to live up to them. Gilbert said it may sound radical, but "if you won't or don't live by our ISMs, you won't work here. We'll still be friends and still say 'hello' in the grocery store, but you won't work here."

And it wasn't just Gilbert who taught the ISMs. Joining him onstage were individuals from across the company and community who exemplified various cultural ISMs and shared inspiring stories and examples that brought them to life. One of the most memorable was Ryan Hudson-Peralta, principal experience designer for Rocket Mortgage and founder of a motivational speaking business called Look Mom No Hands. Ryan speaks worldwide, sharing his experiences and insights from living a full and productive life despite being born with severely shortened arms, no hands, and legs that stopped growing above the knee.[8] As a husband and father, creative director, baseball coach, airplane pilot, and motivational speaker, Ryan exemplifies multiple ISMs and reminds us that having a disability and having ambitions, creativity, and success are not mutually exclusive.

Surprisingly, Gilbert has openly published his ISMs, his secret sauce for building a high-performing culture. He's not worried about other companies replicating his success because he knows how hard it is to get your people to live by your company's desired beliefs and behaviors. The discipline required to consistently teach and model what it looks like to live your company culture requires a deep level of investment across all your leaders at the highest levels of the business.

PURPOSE STATEMENTS WE'VE WRITTEN

SaltStack (configuration management and orchestration tool):
"To amplify the intelligence and impact of every IT professional"

Authentic, Genuine, and Effective

Gathering insights and input from people who deeply care about your company is essential to inform the definition and development of your brand purpose, mission, vision, and values statements. This select group includes company founders, executives, and team members from different departments and levels of responsibility who embody the desired company culture to inform the development of your internal brand story.

Your core values ought to also reflect the attitudes and behaviors that get results. As Roger Connors and Tom Smith teach in their best-selling book, *Change the Culture, Change the Game*, your culture is the way your people need to think and act to consistently achieve your desired outcomes. This was evident at IDEO, where David Kelley and his cofounders, Mike Nuttall and Bill Moggridge, built a meritocracy-based culture where peers decided who was most valuable to the company based on their coworkers' contributions to the firm's legendary ideation sessions and client projects. If you didn't make material contributions to a brainstorm or project, your peers didn't invite you to participate in future opportunities, and you'd eventually find yourself sidelined because no one would pick you to be on their team.

IDEO's founders built a self-correcting culture by hiring world-class talent who shared their belief in human-centered design. Adding value mattered more than title or tenure. Tools like IDEO's seven brainstorming rules (listed below) reinforced a culture where the best ideas won, peers held each other accountable, and individual impact was unmistakable. This approach consistently attracted exceptional people, sparked fresh thinking, and fueled a virtuous cycle of innovation and value creation.

1. Defer Judgment

2. Encourage Wild Ideas

3. Build on the Ideas of Others

4. Stay Focused on the Topic

5. One Conversation at a Time

6. Be Visual

7. Go for Quantity[9]

Like Dan Gilbert, David Kelley, his brother, Tom, and their colleagues at IDEO gave away the innovation design firm's human-centered design methodology in books, speeches, and free content, and, significantly, by forming the Hasso Plattner Institute of Design (informally known as the d.school) at Stanford, which led to the formation of the global design-thinking movement. Their motivations were, at the same time, purposeful for the world and beneficial for the firm. They've given the world a gift by freely sharing IDEO's methods for solving complex problems like illiteracy, malnutrition, and pollution. At the same time, being synonymous with design thinking has burnished IDEO's brand as the best practitioner of this methodology in the world. Giving away IDEO's tools and techniques only helped the firm's reputation grow because those tools are only as valuable as the culture of their practitioners. Ultimately, the most impactful thing IDEO designed and the biggest moat and barrier to would-be competitors isn't found in trademarked terms or patented design or innovation methods. It's baked into the company's culture as one of the best environments anywhere for innovating on demand.

Writing Down the Recipe for Scaling the Magic

Building a great brand and business requires consistently designing and fulfilling compelling customer experiences. Creating these kinds of magical connections can be somewhat accidental and intuitive when your team consists of you as the founder and a couple of other core team members—a pinch of this and a dash of that. But creating a deliberate company culture is the only way to make the magic happen at scale, and to do that, you've got to codify your culture-defining beliefs and behaviors in writing.

If your family is like ours, you probably have some favorite recipes that make your holidays and celebrations more memorable and help reinforce family traditions. Imagine what would happen if the only person in your family who knew how to make these foods was no longer available. You could probably cobble together some semblance of your family favorites, but they wouldn't taste the same as when your mom or grandparents made them—unless they wrote down those recipes for you.

Codifying your culture can start in a variety of ways. The most linear way to do it is by identifying your core values as one-word nouns. Examples include "Collaboration," "Innovation," "Integrity," and "Caring." Articulate the beliefs and behaviors that bring these values to life from there. We'll talk more about this in chapter 12.

PURPOSE STATEMENTS WE'VE WRITTEN

Tanner LLC (accounting and advisory firm):

"To realize the full value of best-in-class teams"

Powerful cultural connections stem from branching out from these root words with the specific beliefs and behaviors that bring your values to life. Generic values statements might as well be invisible. We ignore them because, without meaningful statements and stories to bring them to life, they're forgettable. And the statements that define them must energize people, not like the mass-produced posters we've all seen of a rowing crew gliding across a glassy lake in the early morning mist with a cliché caption about the importance of teamwork. No one notices and no one cares about that kind of mindless material.

In contrast, consider these eleven values or "maxims" reported by LiveAbout that delineate Nike's culture-defining values, consistent with its competitive spirit.

1. It is our nature to innovate.

2. Nike is a company.

3. Nike is a brand.

4. Simplify and go.

5. The consumer decides.

6. Be a sponge.

7. Evolve immediately.

8. Do the right thing.

9. Master the fundamentals.

10. We are on the offense—always.

11. Remember the man [cofounder, Bill Bowerman].[10]

Although these maxims require some explanation and storytelling to bring them to life, they are distinctive and intrinsic to Nike and help reinforce the company's desired culture. Nike places so much value in teaching its culture to its employees that it had a full-time archivist for years who curated a living library of stories and artifacts to share with employees and engage their hearts and minds while transmitting Nike's brand culture.

Core values statements can be customer facing or internal facing, though they're primarily focused on providing attitudinal and behavioral guidelines for employees. In crafting your brand values, a good practice is to imagine your customers reading them online—even though you may not have chosen to make them public—as a test to see if there is anything in your values that you wouldn't want customers to see. An adjunct professor in my grad school program and an important mentor of mine taught us the importance of never making fun of customers out of respect for the people paying the bills. More than being neutral in how we regard and value customers, we need to develop a strong sense of empathy for and with them. Dev Patnaik, founder and CEO of Jump Associates and author of *Wired to Care*, touts empathy as *the* source of differentiated and sustained strategic success. A truly empathetic culture would never make fun of its customers.

PURPOSE STATEMENTS WE'VE WRITTEN

Vasion (workflow management SaaS):

"To make the digital transformation attainable for everyone"

Sharing Your Purpose

Once you have clarified your purpose, created authentic and effective mission, vision, and values statements, and written down your recipe for success by codifying your culture, you have to teach them to your employees over and over again. You'll need to bring your employees, investors, and other stakeholders on board by helping them understand and appreciate the significance and stories behind these things. They need to believe and buy into your purpose so they can make it real for themselves by creating and sharing stories of their own.

CHAPTER 6

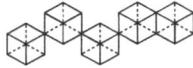

BRAND POSITION

"There's no way to remove the observer—us—
from our perceptions of the world."

—Stephen Hawking

Your brand position consists of the words and ideas customers associate with your brand name. When you think of brand position, think of brand perception. Branding is the process of creating your desired brand perception in customers' minds by using the right kinds of words, images, and experiences in your interactions and relationships with them. If customers don't know your brand exists or don't associate it with the words you want them to, then you don't have a brand or it's not the one you want. You can own your brand name, logo, and tagline, but customers ultimately own your brand because they decide what your brand stands for in their minds, and therefore, they eventually determine the value of your brand.

The Now: Statement of Brand Position

The first step in the brand positioning process is determining what words and ideas customers currently associate with your brand compared to your desired brand perception. Current perceptions define your statement of brand position. *Before you know what changes to make to your brand, you must first understand how customers perceive it today.*

If you have an established business, you can determine your statement of brand position by identifying your ideal customers, the kind you'd love to have more of, and asking them what comes to mind when they think of your brand name and why. These should be real customers who have already bought from you, not too-good-to-be-true customers who don't exist or are rare in the real world. There should be enough of them to constitute a sizable, total addressable market (TAM) opportunity for you and your business.

As discussed previously, it's important to gather perspectives from a representative cross-section of your most valuable customer segments, which we define as groups of people who buy for the same reasons and talk to one another. If you are building a new brand that doesn't have any customers, talk with prospective customers who represent the market segments you believe will find your offerings relevant and valuable, even if those customers are currently using alternative solutions today.

The Future: Brand Positioning Statement

To change your brand from its current perception to the one you want, you need to make intentional, deliberate, and consistent choices to reinforce your desired brand perception from the customer's point of view. You need to determine the words and ideas you want to be synonymous with your brand in your customers' minds. The answers to these questions define your brand positioning statement, a concise declaration of how you want customers to perceive your brand in the future. Your business or product may already live up to your desired brand perception, or you may have some innovative work to do to close your brand gap to make your desired perception true. Either way, you've got to make your brand reality match up with your desired brand perception.

In his classic marketing book *Crossing the Chasm*, Geoffrey Moore provides the following framework as a guide for writing brand positioning statements by filling in the blanks with your answers:

For (target customer) who (statement of the need or opportunity),
the (product name) is a (product category)
that (statement of key benefit—a compelling reason to buy).
Unlike (the primary competitive alternative),
our product (statement of primary definition).[1]

Of course, your answers to these basic questions should be informed by real insights gleaned from enlightened conversations with real customers, not assumptions or the opinions of the loudest or most dogmatic voices in your conference room.

Traditionally, management consultants, brand strategists, and product managers have used simple frameworks, like a two-by-two matrix, to visually represent how brands are positioned—or want to be positioned—relative to one another. The Gartner Magic Quadrant is an example of a two-by-two positioning matrix based on completeness of vision and ability to execute.

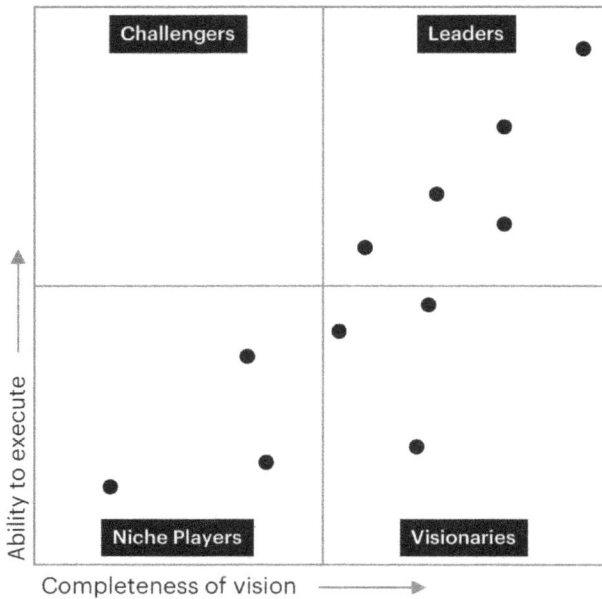

Challengers

Leaders

Ability to execute

Niche Players

Visionaries

Completeness of vision

(Source: Gartner, "Gartner Magic Quadrant,"
https://www.gartner.co.uk/en/methodologies/magic-quadrants-research.)

Within a two-by-two positioning framework, the goal is to position your brand as a leader in its category, with the most coveted position being in the upper-right-hand corner of the upper-right-hand quadrant. Claiming a desirable market position on your own is one thing. Getting credible third parties—industry experts, analysts, and, most importantly, customers—to say it for you requires compelling evidence in the form of a clear vision, customer case studies, and measurable business results. Winning over industry pundits can take years of validating your claims with a consistent and compelling body of work. It may require you to share the stage with influential opinion leaders who make a living out of defining categories and crowning their winners.

The two-by-two matrix approach is a simple, straightforward way to think about how to position your brand for success while depositioning your competition. Still, two-by-two matrixes have limitations as they only provide a two-dimensional perspective on positioning your product or brand. Brands that aim to truly disrupt an industry or category craft a strategic narrative that frames their value within the context of a major market shift, fuels their strategy, and highlights their strengths.

Bridging the Gap

The gap between your current brand perception, we'll call it P1, and your desired brand perception, we'll call it P2, is your brand perception gap. Closing this gap is the essence of developing an effective brand strategy. It defines the words, images, and experiences required to successfully influence customers' perceptions of your brand. You may not be able to control what customers think of your brand, but you can influence their perceptions.

What appears to be beautiful to the right customers might not land with others. Ensuring your brand makes the right first impressions on the right customers is crucial because getting them to change their

perceptions later on is difficult, if not impossible. Also, it's important to think about what you want your brand to be known for long-term—from the beginning—so you don't box yourself in by making early moves that create narrow perceptions in your customers' minds.

FROM/TO

In its simplest form, the brand positioning process can be stated as going from a current perception to a new one. As discussed in chapter 4, a simple From/To table can help organize your thoughts. By listing current brand perceptions in the left-hand column and contrasting the desired perception in the right-hand column, you make the before-and-after positioning picture easier to understand and share with your team.

A nonprofit organization called VentureCapital.Org asked us to guide them through a rebrand. The organization was approaching its fortieth anniversary of mentoring first-time startup founders and showing them how to validate, package, and pitch their business ideas to early-stage investors. Despite the organization's longevity, it was diluting its brand position and perception by sending mixed signals to stakeholders.

The organization's name confused state legislators, among others; some mistakenly thought it was a for-profit venture capital fund and couldn't understand why it would ask for state dollars to help grow new businesses and create more jobs. Similarly, the organization's name led some entrepreneurs to think VentureCapital.Org could be a source of funding for them, which wasn't the case. Mentors saw the organization as a way to make new professional connections while giving back and sharing their expertise. Investors were starting to identify with and revolve around the organization's sub-brand events as though they were the parent brand itself.

Like the famous Indian parable of the blind men and the elephant,

VentureCapital.Org stood for something different to each of its audiences. It lacked a clear brand position its audiences could buy into and identify with, promote, and support.

Based on our findings from the Brand Discovery process, we uncovered insights into narrative themes and threads true to the brand's origin story, acknowledged positive developments in becoming more inclusive of women and minorities, resonated with all its stakeholder groups, and paved the way for new growth opportunities. We leveraged these insights to position the brand from an organization with a fuzzy and confused image to "A nonprofit organization that makes entrepreneurs more investable and connects them to capital in underserved markets across the U.S."

In support of this new positioning statement, we changed the name of the organization from VentureCapital.Org—a name chosen for its domain availability—to Kinect Capital. The new name reinforced the organization's origin story as one of America's first accelerators while renewing its heartfelt commitment to creating a sense of kinship and community where entrepreneurs, mentors, and investors connect.

KINECT CAPITAL REBRAND	
From: Statement of Position	To: Positioning Statement
A confusing name that implies venture capital	A name that communicates kinship, community, and connection
An old boys club	An inclusive community
A portfolio of disconnected events	A strong solar system of related brands with the Kinect brand at the center
An outdated image	A vibrant, vital identity

By clarifying its brand position and changing its name, the organization reaffirmed its nonprofit status and positioned the parent brand as paramount. Placed at the center of the Kinect Capital universe, all its event brands revolved around the parent company as strong subsidiaries and satellites.

NAMING YOUR BRAND

Choosing the right brand name is one of the most important considerations in creating your desired brand perception. It's not uncommon for brands to start out serving one audience with a narrow brand name only to later realize they want to pursue a bigger market opportunity requiring a different brand name. Such was the case with a SaaS company I worked for called DemoChimp.

Initially, the company focused on marketing and selling its demo automation software to small- and medium-sized businesses (SMBs). As time passed and the company matured, it gained traction with midsized and enterprise organizations. The company's original tongue-in-cheek DemoChimp name sounded fun and clever when the business was young and focused on serving SMBs, but when the business began to pivot into selling enterprise deals, its playful name caused prospective enterprise customers to question whether the company could meet their needs at scale.

Since the company's brand promise was to facilitate consensus among all the participants involved in making buying decisions on behalf of large organizations, I suggested we rename the company from DemoChimp to Consensus, which we did. The new name didn't turn off SMBs, and it helped legitimize the brand with large enterprise organizations. The new name also suggests what the company's software does as another way to reinforce its unique selling proposition (USP).

Since its name change, Consensus has gone on to create a new category and establish itself as the leader in demo automation software, helping presales leaders and big businesses make it easier for customers to buy from them.

Along with ensuring your name fits your audience's size, scale, and personality, it's important to remember that we say and hear brand names more often than we look at them. Giving too much weight to how a brand name looks in a professionally designed logo when evaluating naming alternatives is a mistake. It's more important to consider how names sound to people and the ease with which they can spell and remember them when evaluating potential options.

The best time to rename and rebrand your business is when it's small and relatively unknown rather than having to do it later when it's already put down roots and is spreading its branches, filling out, and thriving. We'll talk more about different kinds of names later, but naming is definitely an essential part of brand positioning.

CATEGORY CREATION

It's not uncommon for clients to talk with us about creating a new category. Defining a new space and being the first brand to enter that category sounds bold and exciting, but creating a new category takes a lot of work, sustained focus, energy, effort, and investment over a long period time. Naming a new category doesn't necessarily make your category matter or make you the leader of it. It often takes five to ten years to create a new category and gain adoption from customers, analysts, and industry experts. It takes time for them to understand, appreciate, and embrace a new category—then associate your brand with it and, ideally, recognize it as the category's leader.

The prevailing wisdom is the first brand to define and lead a new category ends up owning the biggest piece of it, even after other competitors have entered the new space. Having competitors join the party is necessary to legitimize the relevance of the category; owning a smaller slice of a growing pie is often worth more than having a small pie all to yourself.

In their category-defining book, *Play Bigger*, authors Dave Peterson, Al Ramadan, and Christopher Lochhead teach the importance of designing a company, product, and category all at the same time. They teach that new categories are born out of a new insight into a market need or technology that reframes and promotes the problem and opportunity to solve it in a *different*, not just *better*, way.

A complementary concept from *The Challenger Customer*, by authors Brent Adamson, Matthew Dixon, Pat Spenner, and Nick Toman, reiterates the importance of leading *to* your solution, not *with* it. By promoting the problem your new category or solution solves, you're creating more awareness and demand for it among would-be customers and framing the criteria they ought to use in shopping for an answer—criteria only your solution completely satisfies.

At Consensus, we made the market aware of hours of wasted time and missed opportunities created by one-size-fits-all software demonstrations and how much the status quo was costing them. Garin Hess, the company's insightful founder and CEO, reframed the problem in terms of the buying process being too hard. He made a compelling case for the buyer enablement solutions in articles, industry presentations, and his book *Selling Is Hard, Buying Is Harder*, stating it's harder for customers to buy than it is for salespeople to sell. Based on these insights, Garin pivoted the business to focus with laser-like precision on presales engineers. The company has experienced significant growth after reframing and promoting the buyer enablement problem and positioning itself as the leader in solving it.

BRANDING PROGRESSION AND SUSTAINABILITY

Foundational principles of brand positioning include branding progression and sustainability. The stepping-stone career steps Will Smith took in building his professional brand made sense. He went from high school rapper to TV actor, movie actor, movie star, and producer. Smith had to demonstrate he was doing the work necessary to earn each progressive title and brand perception. For example, had Smith claimed to be a movie producer when he was a rapper, no one would have believed him.

Once you've established your desired brand perception, you've got to reinforce it by retaining and supporting those positive associations. In a flash of emotion, Smith hurt his brand by slapping Chris Rock onstage at the Oscars. Going from rapper to slapper probably wasn't the narrative arc Smith had in mind for his brand when he started his journey. Reputations that take years to build can tumble in a momentary lapse of control or good judgment. We must continue providing our audiences with differentiated and relevant words, images, and experiences to reinforce our desired brand perceptions even after our brand names have become synonymous with the ideas and words we want customers to associate us with in their minds.

BRAND EXTENSIONS

When customers associate your brand with a specific category of attributes and benefits, there are limits to how far it can extend from its original anchor point and still be relevant. That's another reason it's so important to be intentional and think carefully about your brand impression early on, particularly for your customers. Rewiring the connections customers have made between your brand name and their perceptions of it is nearly impossible once those perceptions are fully formed.

FedEx, for example, imprinted itself on the hearts and minds of the market by being the first brand associated with overnight shipping. Even though FedEx has added many other kinds of services to its lineup, its origin story and legendary ad campaigns have their roots in being the first overnight shipping company. Aside from generational turnover, brand perceptions often persist for a long time.

UNINTENDED USE CASES AND RESONANCE

Sometimes, we think we know in advance which audiences will embrace the new products and services we're bringing to market and how they will put those products to use, but we may be surprised to learn the market has other ideas. For example, Andrew Abraham, MD, founder and creator of Orgain, the organic protein shake, thought his product would be popular as a more nutritious alternative to products like Ensure nutritional supplements for patients in hospitals and those unable to eat solid foods for medical reasons. Instead, many people started using it as meal replacements on the go, taking his business in a different, though highly profitable, direction.

CONTEXT IS KING

The same product can be positioned and perceived differently depending on contextualization. For example, oranges can be positioned as a breakfast drink, a vitamin, a garnish, a holiday gift, an air freshener and deodorizer, a natural cleaner, or a skin rub. Different people can have entirely different perceptions of the same product depending on how it's presented to them or how their culture has integrated it into their lifestyle. SPAM means something entirely different to the people of Hawaii, who incorporated the luncheon meat into their everyday culture after GIs introduced it to them in World War II, than it does to someone on the mainland receiving unwanted email. All the more reason to be crystal clear about who your customers are and the problems you're solving for them as you map your brand strategy.

REASONS TO BELIEVE

For your desired brand position to be believable, you must support the claims you make on behalf of your brand with credible evidence. Before customers believe in your product or service, they must have a successful experience themselves or receive and resonate with endorsements from credible customers. Customer reviews can help prospective customers build enough belief in your product or service, but not all customer reviews and testimonials carry equal weight. Depending on the customer segment, getting an endorsement from a particularly respected thought leader in their industry might make all the difference. One solid and sincere endorsement from the right customer can put your brand on the map and keep it there if your brand performs as promised.

BY ASSOCIATION

The people and other brands with which you associate your brand will reflect on and shape everyone's perception of it. Indiscriminately accepting offers to collaborate with other brands, individuals, or big businesses can muddy customer perceptions of your brand, or worse, compromise and damage their perceptions of your brand outright. Strategic partnerships and collaborative ventures can add accretive value to your brand by positive associations from their brands rubbing off on yours. Being selective is the way to go, and having strategic branding parameters and guiding principles makes the selection process more manageable and scalable for growing teams.

BRAND STEWARDSHIP

You need clarity about your desired brand position and a long-term commitment to bringing it to fruition, or you'll lose your way. Without a robust brand strategy, strong-willed leaders and ambitious creative directors can take your brand down a shortsighted path, indulging their personal preferences or career ambitions at the expense of building focused brand equity with employees, customers, partners, and shareholders over time.

When your organization has a shared sense of who you are and how you want to be perceived, you can channel the strategic and creative energies of leaders and strong personalities to produce better outcomes for your brand and business now and in the future. You can help whoever is at the ship's helm steer it on course during their watch as a responsible steward who uses whatever headwinds come your way to tack toward your strategic brand destination instead of letting those headwinds blow you off course.

Reframe the Narrative

Creating a strategic brand narrative can elevate your brand positioning from a red ocean feature-benefit fistfight to finding your blue ocean space and sailing in clear air. It can help you close the gap between your current and desired perception in a big way. Although the applications vary from one practitioner and framework to another, the guiding principles for setting your brand apart with a compelling narrative remain the same.

Principle 1. Make your customer the center of your story: Remember the hero of your brand story is your customer, not your company. Don't assume your customer is aware of the need for change or feels compelled to do something about it.

Principle 2. Show your customers how their world has changed by creating a problem they can't afford to ignore: Andy Raskin, the successful Silicon Valley startup advisor, says you should frame your strategic narrative in the context of a big, relevant, undeniable change to which your customers must adapt to come out on top and not be left behind. A compatible concept comes from technology analyst firm Corporate Executive Board (CEB), now part of Gartner, recommending that you lead *to* your solution, not *with* it, in their book *The Challenger Customer*, sequel to *The Challenger Sale*. After researching what successful enterprise marketing and sales teams do, CEB found that the most effective marketing strategies start by promoting a customer problem that is so costly that staying the same is greater than the pain of making a change.

Principle 3. Show customers what life could be like with their problem solved: Raskin advocates giving customers a glimpse of the promised land to which you can lead them by sharing examples of the world you're creating. He suggests showing them what life will be like with your offering without talking directly about your product or service. It should be presented as a desirable vision of the new world nearly impossible to achieve without your help. CEB suggests creating compelling case studies linking your solution to resolving an acute customer pain point in a quantifiable way.

The process starts by thinking about what customers ultimately want and linking your solution to it with clearly defined cause-and-effect connections. For example, *The Challenger Customer* includes a case study where Dentsply reframed the value of its new cordless hygienist handpiece for dentists by showing how it was the solution to carpal tunnel syndrome among hygienists resulting from corded hand-pieces, a problem that led to high absenteeism and downward pressure on production and profitability in dental practices. Keep in mind that you can't fabricate a desired perception merely by telling your customers what they want to hear; you have to fulfill your promises and truly solve problems that matter to them.

Principle 4. Define the criteria for success on terms only you can satisfy: Raskin advocates talking about your features in terms of how they help your customer get to their promised land, providing evidence along the way that you can make it come true. CEB talks about defining the criteria only your brand can satisfy for solving your customer's problem. With these ideas in mind, we recommend clarifying and articulating your five most significant differentiators and the benefits they provide, which we refer to as your brand pillars. For this approach to be effective, none of your competitors ought to be able to satisfy all five of the success criteria.

CHAPTER 7

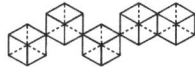

BRAND PROMISE

"Price is what you pay. Value is what you get."

—Warren Buffett

A t its most basic, building a brand is making and keeping a meaningful promise at scale. Your brand promise is the overarching value you deliver to customers—*overarching* meaning your brand promise is audience-agnostic. This type of messaging is different from benefit statements—also known as marketing messages, value propositions, or unique selling propositions (USPs)—that are audience or offering specific. Benefit statements succinctly summarize why people buy your product or service; in other words, what's in it for them. They simply state a problem or benefit customers get from using your offerings. A well-crafted brand promise is a meta-benefit statement that resonates with all your audiences all at once—that is music to their ears regardless of their unique pain points and reasons for buying.

The Brand Discovery process, along with the insights it uncovers into the cumulative pain points and problems solved with your offerings, helps you understand what to promise as well as how to communicate your promise in a way that meaningfully and memorably resonates with your audience. Naturally, your brand promise is broader than narrowly-focused messaging that targets specific audiences because your brand promise is inclusive of everyone in your ecosystem of value. The more products your brand offers and audiences you serve, the broader your brand promise must be to wrap its arms around all of them. The opposite is also true—if you serve only one audience with just a single or few offerings, your brand promise can be much narrower in scope.

After completing dozens of customer interviews for Lucidchart, our combined project team delivered a messaging framework that matched dozens of customer pain points with product features and benefits according to different customer segments and use cases. In reviewing the individual benefits, the company aggregated them in a single over-arching brand promise for all its audiences: "Bring teams together to make better decisions and build the future." Clicking on the Solutions tab of the company's website further explains how the product does so with audience-specific benefit statements.

The primary benefit of Lucidchart, specific to software engineers, is to *understand and communicate complex ideas*. For IT people, the benefit is to *optimize your processes and infrastructure*. For product leaders, Lucidchart can help *communicate your product vision*. For operations folks, the benefit is to *increase efficiency and transparency*. In addition to departmental benefits, Lucidchart's website communicates how its solution helps everyone *improve processes, optimize organizations, visualize technical systems,* and *replace Visio* regardless of where they sit in an organization. Each benefit statement is tailored to a specific audience and pain point.

We worked with Grow at three different inflection points in its growth and progression over six years as the company continued to scale and expand its iterative understanding of who its customers were and what they wanted in a mature product offering. Informed and inspired by insights from the company's founder, Rob Nelson, along with customer interviews and ongoing competitive analysis, we helped the company summarize its overarching value, which it expresses today as "Lead with data."

Grow's brand promise is all the more significant because Grow's business model and pricing approach make it affordable for everyone in their customers' organizations to be able to use Grow's business intelligence SaaS platform. The business model is in direct contrast to competitors whose traditional seat-by-seat licensing agreements make it too costly and challenging for many businesses to give access to those beyond the C-suite and their direct reports.

For Tanner, Utah's premiere independent public accounting firm, the challenge was to summarize an overarching brand promise and value proposition spanning an extensive and expanding portfolio of practice areas while helping deposition the competition, including local accounting firms and the local offices of national firms like EY, Deloitte, and KPMG. The brand promise we crafted for Tanner—"Get the right answers, right here"—reminds clients and prospective clients alike that Tanner has the capability of national firms to solve complex business issues, plus the autonomy and authority of a local firm. Tanner's promise reiterates the idea that it can swim in the deep end of the pool from a strategic planning and technical know-how perspective, like the Big

Four. Moreover, it doesn't have to defer to a senior officer from an out-of-state office (who doesn't know local clients and whose first thought is how to protect their firm) to sign off on financial statements. With Tanner, there is no "corporate."

Make a Promise You Can Keep

Finding the right words for your brand promise is only half the challenge; the other half, which can be a lot more difficult, is consistently living up to and fulfilling the commitments those words represent. It's always better to make a more modest promise than overstating what you can do and falling down on those commitments.

When Havenpark Communities, the manufactured homes owner-operator, approached us about helping it build a brand that stood out in its industry, our first thought was to find out what made the company truly different and relevant to its audiences. Havenpark does different things and does things differently than other companies in its space. For starters, Havenpark makes significant capital expenditure (CapEx) investments to improve its communities by repaving roads, installing street signs, and maintaining community centers, common areas, playgrounds, and swimming pools. We saw examples of these improvements firsthand when we visited seven Havenpark communities in four different states. We also saw the improvements Havenpark was making in its acquired properties. In contrast, we saw communities owned by other operators in similar areas that were in disrepair.

We spoke with Havenpark residents who had diligently done their part to create a warm and welcoming community despite previous owners' indifference and lack of support. One woman told us she and another resident carried water in buckets—by hand—to keep the flowers and trees alive on the main road into their community when the owner failed to repair broken sprinkler lines. She was committed to making her community a respectable place to live in part because her middle-school kids were getting teased by their classmates for living in a "trailer park." When the bus dropped them off after school, her son and daughter walked toward the mobile home park on the right while the other kids walked toward the large homes on the left. As a single mom, she had worked hard to earn her associate's degree in interior design, and her kids' friends were surprised at how nice their home looked when they finally came over to visit after school one day. Once Havenpark took over the property where this woman lived, the external community environment began to match her carefully curated interior home environment.

And it wasn't just how the neighborhood looked—it was how it *felt*. Another resident talked about how much it meant when he'd returned from working the swing shift at his manufacturing job and his neighbor had shoveled the snow from his driveway and taken his garbage cans to the curb. These simple neighborly acts made him feel like he lived in a *real* community, not just a mobile home park. Stories like these kept surfacing in our Brand Discovery interviews and conversations, letting us know residents in Havenpark's properties valued living in communities that cared.

Havenpark also backs up its community managers in holding all residents accountable for honoring community guidelines and showing one another respect. One community manager shared how a resident had been verbally abusive to her when he didn't like the previous owner's change in policy. She didn't feel she could stand up for herself because the previous owner was too worried about holding on to all its residents. Havenpark is so committed to everyone treating one another with respect in their communities, they're willing to hold residents accountable for mistreating employees, even if it means some residents move on. Clearly, Havenpark is sincerely committed to making improvements and cultivating healthy relationships. In a word, it cares.

In addition to seeing these improvements, we interviewed residents and managers to find out what it's like to live and work in a Havenpark community. They told us what matters most to them is respect. They want to live in a community that respects them. These observations and conversations pointed to an inspirational and motivational brand promise: "Belong to a caring community." The company loved how the promise speaks to and resonates with internal audiences of employees and investors as well as external audiences, including residents, community managers, surrounding communities, and municipalities.

The company's only hesitation in adopting the brand promise was concern about whether it could consistently live up to it. As much as the founders loved their newly articulated and differentiated brand promise, they acknowledged they were still a young company and needed to put some additional operational infrastructure, systems, and processes in place to ensure their entire team across all their locations could live up to their promise before taking it to market. The founders held their promise in reserve for a few months while implementing those structural changes, then brought their brand story and promise to market with complete confidence, knowing they could fulfill it.

In addition to helping Havenpark articulate a heartfelt brand promise, we also facilitated the process of assisting it in defining its brand culture, including the beliefs and behaviors it expected its employees to live by to live up to its brand promise. Havenpark embraced the brand culture process so much it has integrated it into its employee reviews, promotions, and compensation program. As a result, Havenpark has attracted better talent, more investment, and higher occupancy rates in its communities in the process of creating caring communities across America.

Elevate the Right Benefit

A good way to develop your promise is to first write all the benefit statements for your specific products and audiences and then look for one benefit you can elevate. Remember, your brand promise should resonate with everyone you serve. To test your brand promise, circle back to each of your audiences and see if it works for them. You can do this informally by thinking through it yourself and discussing it with your team, or you can test your brand promise with customers to see if it resonates with them. Validating your brand promise with real customers is always the best way to go, though methods vary depending on your resources. It's essential to get feedback from customers who represent your ideal market segments and to ensure they give you their sincere opinions and perceptions.

Dovetail Fit

Your brand promise should align with and build on your brand purpose and position. These elements of your Brand Foundation should neatly fit together, like a dovetail joint in a fine piece of furniture—never forced. When you put your Brand Foundation together, if you find yourself with extra parts left over or feel like you need to pound on your promise to make it fit—it's not right yet.

Don't be surprised if you think you've found your brand promise only to come back later to refine it. As with all the foundational elements of your brand, clarifying and articulating your brand promise is an iterative process. In defining the elements of your brand, you may need to make further adjustments so everything goes together seamlessly.

Remember to consider the vision of your organization as you write your brand promise. While it's essential to describe your brand's most important and universally applicable value proposition to reflect the total value of what you deliver today, it's equally important to consider how your meta value proposition may change in the future. You'll want to describe your current brand promise in a way that aligns with your future brand vision in your brand narrative.

Sometimes, brands need to anticipate what they want to be when they grow up to successfully brand themselves for the present. You can avoid costly mistakes by thinking ahead regarding your brand's ultimate destination and making today's branding decisions in alignment with your long-term goals.

Watch Your Language

Writing your brand promise in the imperative mood creates a command or request. We default to this style of writing because it's relatively simple and straightforward and helps your customers realize the significance of your brand promise and how it benefits their businesses.

For example, when we worked with Cadence Homes, a semicustom home builder, we wrote a brand promise to highlight the overarching benefit it provides customers—giving them more options than cookie-cutter tract home builders—with a simple, direct brand promise that says it all in just four words: "Build what you want." This was the most concise way to summarize the unique business model Cadence designed—letting its customers make more changes to their homes to better reflect their individual styles and personalities. Making this bold and credible claim helped Cadence command a premium for their semicustom homes because delivering more value doesn't make sense unless your customers give you credit for it.

However, imperative mood isn't the only way to write a benefit statement or a brand promise because there are times when it may not be appropriate for a given audience. Using the present participle form of the verb, which adds -ing to the root word, will soften your promise, making it sound more like a suggestion than an imperative command. In working with a client in the agriculture industry, we quickly learned farmers (growers) do not appreciate brands telling them what to do or implying they've been doing something inadequately. Considering this cultural preference, we changed the company's original brand promise from the imperative mood, "Make your farm 10 to 20 percent more efficient," to the present participle form, "Helping farms be 10 to 20 percent more efficient." This subtle shift changed the statement from a command that the customer change their behavior to emphasizing that the company is continually providing a valuable service.

Reasons to Believe

As obvious as this sounds, providing reasons to believe (RTB) is still worth stating here because brands can paint themselves into a corner if they overlook them. Your business must back what it promises customers with a credible reason to believe or, better yet, reasons to believe. Your RTBs can include customer testimonials, awards, the number of years you've been in business, or, in the case of McDonald's restaurants, the billions and billions of customers they've served. Before you enthrone your brand promise, ensure you've got the right RTBs to back it with your audiences.

Remember not to overreach or overstate what you can do. It's one thing to point to where your software is going to be in another six to twelve months while you're building out the next version, but to boldly claim to do something you can't or won't do today or for a long time to come is just plain wrong. Brands that play this game eventually pay for it. We've all seen examples of this play out in the news cycle when yet another politician is caught cheating on their resume, but it goes even further. More and more academics at acclaimed universities have been found fudging the numbers to support their research findings. We live in an increasingly transparent world where no one can get away with overstating their value for very long.

Sequence Matters

Building your Brand Foundation is a sequential process. You can't write your brand promise until *after* you've written your brand purpose and position; they're interconnected. If you get the steps out of order, your Brand Foundation will be disjointed and unstable. Also, unlike your timeless brand purpose, you'll want to refresh your brand position and brand promise periodically as you bring new offerings to market, expand your audiences, and anticipate and respond to changes in the competitive landscape.

In making the transition from one brand promise to the next, it's crucial to remember that existing customers remember your brand history. They know where you came from, what you stood for, and what you meant to them in the past, so if your brand has a history—good or bad—don't pretend like it doesn't. If you're doing a complete rebrand, which includes a new brand name, consider your brand's positive equity and look for ways to carry it forward with your new brand.

Front and Center

Experienced brands typically communicate their brand promises in the first sections of their website home pages "above the fold"—without requiring visitors to scroll down. They quickly communicate their highest order of value because they know it's unsafe to assume site visitors will read beyond that first statement of value. However, there is a good chance prospective customers will read on if they see value in the first headline and blurb.

Rather than entrusting this all-important statement to a copywriter who may or may not be familiar with your audiences and the value your brand provides, it's of the utmost importance that you deliberately define your brand promise to communicate in a clear, concise, consistent way across customer touch points.

Be Clear

Making a meaningful promise and consistently keeping it is the essence of building a big brand. A brand promise is a clear, concise benefit statement communicating the overarching value you deliver to all your customers. Typically, benefit statements are written in the imperative mood, starting with a verb that sounds like a command, giving customers a sense of confidence and urgency in realizing the promised benefit of your offerings. In thinking about and writing your brand promise, remember to adjust its level of specificity to reflect the breadth of all your audiences. The broader and more diverse your audiences' needs are, the broader your brand promise will be.

CHAPTER 8

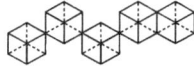

BRAND PILLARS

"In order to be irreplaceable, one must always be different."

—**Coco Chanel**

Having defined your brand purpose, position, and promise, you've laid a strong Brand Foundation for building. The next step in developing your brand is to set forth your brand pillars—the five most significant reasons you win. Your pillars are your five biggest differentiators along with the main benefits customers derive from each one. Your brand pillars make a case for why customers should prefer and choose your offering over alternatives. Done well, they define a set of compelling criteria customers should use in shopping for a solution to their problem and that you alone can satisfy.

As discussed previously, you can generate demand for your offering by marketing the problem you solve and quantifying the cost of not doing anything about it. Other companies may be able to meet some of the criteria but not all. If you haven't found your fantastic five, rethink the ones you have or innovate and develop new differentiators no one else can credibly claim. By framing your five factors of success this way, you lead *to* your solution, not *with* it, a crucial marketing strategy given the abundance of information customers access online to educate themselves before ever talking with you.

Framing your customer's buying decisions in the context of the five success criteria that favor your solution will be effective only if the criteria are truly necessary for customer success and your solution satisfies them all. What you advocate and claim has to be accurate and relevant. If the selection criteria you put out into the world aren't essential or your offering can't truly satisfy them, your words will fall flat, or worse, you will break trust with your customers and undermine the credibility of your brand.

Stand-Out Criteria

Defining five criteria for success is manageable and gives you the needed factors to set your offering apart. Five factors are also easy to teach because you can count them on one hand onstage or on a Zoom call as a convenient memory and speaking device. There will likely be competitors who can satisfy some of your success criteria. Still, if you've identified the right factors, none of your competitors should be able to meet them all or trump them with even more relevant factors you can't match. If they can, you may need to look closer at your product and service development strategy and find new ways to innovate.

Your five pillars form the basis of your content marketing strategy. Like the menu at Taco Bell, you can repeatedly use the same five ingredients in different configurations to solve the problem you're marketing and use it for various audiences and communication channels. Your five pillars provide the outline for any content you might want to create, including keynote presentations, sales presentations, investor presentations, website copy, ads, webinars, blog posts, social media posts, media interviews, and more. Instead of scrambling to throw something together at the last minute, you can feel calm, confident, and collected, knowing you know what to say in any communication situation.

We worked with a performance marketing agency, Disruptive Advertising, to differentiate its offering, culture, approach, and messaging from their would-be competitors. The agency has one of the best reputations for getting results for clients and is consistently ranked as the top pay-per-click (PPC) advertising and SEO firm based on hundreds of glowing client testimonials. It's also in the top 1 percent of Google Ads agencies, having spent over $1 billion on Google ads, not to mention being the "#1 Most Reviewed Marketing Agency Across Review Platforms."

As its name suggests, Disruptive Advertising is disrupting the traditional way of doing business by being the most authentic marketing partner in the industry. As the agency continued to grow and mature, not everyone on the team could consistently and concisely articulate what set it apart, leaving money and opportunities on the table in its efforts to attract new team members and clients. In consultation with Jake Baadsgaard, Disruptive's founder and CEO, we identified and succinctly articulated the five criteria that set the agency apart as well as the five most significant benefits clients received from them.

These differentiators gave Jake the clarity he needed to teach his team how to share the agency's story in a way that made it more apparent to prospective team members and clients that Disruptive was different and relevant. They helped the agency attract like-minded talent and clients, thus preserving and enhancing its unique culture of authenticity and its leadership position.

Of course, differentiation is a never-ending process. None of us is immune to competitive pressure to continue to innovate. Coasting will cost you the ability to remain relevant as new entrants and competitors continue to push the state of the art forward. That's why Jake and his team continue finding new ways to add value.

FIND YOUR PILLARS

Identifying the five most important success factors is a blend of thinking about what customers need to succeed and what sets your offering apart. Disruptive developed its pillars by reflecting on the factors that attracted, converted, and retained its most valuable clients, the ones it wanted to have more of. The agency deconstructed its most valued and beloved client relationships to identify the elements of its offering that resonated with those specific clients. Specifically, we worked with the company's founder to draft a list of five factors that set the agency apart. After letting those ideas cure for a week or so, we returned to them and, with the help of other longtime leaders at the agency, further refined them until they fit neatly together and supported the overarching structure of the Brand Foundation.

Then we expanded the circle of collaboration to include other insightful participants from different areas across the agency's leadership team who reviewed and ratified them as worthy of putting in front of clients. Members of the expanded Disruptive team began using them in marketing and sales activities to promote the agency and watched for signs of resonance or rejection. In combination with Alex Hormozi's *$100M Offers* methodology, the messaging we developed with Jake and his team resulted in record-setting revenues for the agency along with a reduction in the cost and time required to acquire new clients.

As the pillars performed well, the agency put its full weight behind them and adopted them wholesale. The five factors we ended up with were these:

1. **Authenticity:** We only work with people and brands we believe in.

2. **Top Talent:** We hire, develop, and retain top talent you can trust.

3. **Strategy:** We align the right business goals to the right marketing strategy.

4. **Breakthroughs:** We leverage people, tools, and technology to deliver breakthrough results.

5. **Exclusivity:** We provide access to exclusive relationships, content, and community.

A helpful exercise to facilitate this process is creating a simple value curve chart in Microsoft Excel or Google Sheets that shows what customers want in a solution for a particular problem and scoring your offering's ability to satisfy those needs compared to competitors' offerings. At this stage, don't worry about narrowing down the number of features in your analysis to fit within a five-factor limit. Let your ideas flow initially and capture all potential candidate features. You can down-select the most significant features after unpacking all possible options.

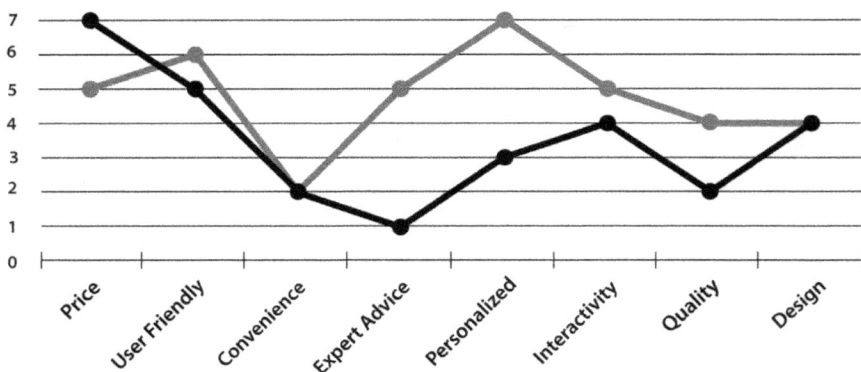

Of equal importance to identifying your differentiators is explicitly communicating the benefits they provide customers. If you're not intentional, you may simply list aspects or attributes of your products and services without clearly stating how they make life better for customers. It's up to you to tell your customers out loud what they will get from your products and services. You can't leave it up to customers to extrapolate why they should care about your offering having one feature or another. They may draw the wrong conclusions or be too busy and distracted to figure it out. Left on their own, they may not see or appreciate the connection between what your offering does, how it does it, and how that could help them solve their problems in satisfying ways.

Remember, a brand pillar in and of itself is incomplete. One of your brand's most significant features, a pillar has broad application to all your audiences. Unless you pair a pillar (super feature) with a super important benefit, customers may miss the "what's in it for me" moment. You've got to make the main benefit of each pillar so obvious that customers don't misinterpret the benefit or miss it altogether. Simply stating a pillar is asking too much of your audience; you've got to tell them why they should care and why they should buy in the form of an effective and compelling benefit statement. Limit yourself to one primary benefit per pillar to keep it simple for you and your team to compellingly argue why customers should select your offering. Simplicity also helps your team avoid getting tangled up in too many details.

THE BIGGER THE MOAT, THE BETTER

The bigger the separation between what you can uniquely claim between your five factors of success and what your competitors have to offer, the better. It's advantageous to focus on features of your offering that are most difficult for competitors to match. The best differentiators are structurally significant; they're baked into an aspect of your business model that is difficult, if not impossible, for competitors to replicate without investing a lot of time, energy, and financial resources. Better yet, build a moat they can't cross from a patent or trade secret perspective, a protective barrier they can't work around that will last a long time.

Brands can be effective moats in and of themselves if they become synonymous with a category or idea in customers' minds that is impossible to uproot and replace. Our client, Gabb, achieved this resonance by being first to market with the "Safe tech for kids" message we helped them articulate. Then Gabb continued to back it up with ongoing product introductions that solved real problems for parents who wanted to stay safely connected to their tweens.

You may find opportunities to leverage naturally occurring moats. The tidal waters surrounding Mont-Saint-Michel in Normandy, France, have protected it for centuries. If you opportunistically discover or acquire a strategic differentiator, like a new trademark or technology, leverage it to the fullest extent possible in fortifying your brand pillars.

If your assumptions about a moat fail to materialize or they morph on you, quickly make a change and move on to better options. Edward I dug a deep moat around the Tower of London and let sewage from the castle run into it—water from the River Thames was then supposed to flush it out through sluice gates. The moat worked well until the mid-1840s when the animal and human waste stench and disease became unbearable at low tide. Since then, the moat has been filled in, leaving a wide-open area that has struggled to find a meaningful purpose even as the tower has become one of London's most popular tourist attractions.[1]

LOAD TESTING

In the 1930s, when Frank Lloyd Wright received the commission to design the headquarters for the SC Johnson company in Racine, Wisconsin, people doubted the ability of the lily pad columns he specified to support the roof and building. Wright proved his unique pillar design would work by loading twenty-four tons of sand on the top of a test column without cracking the pillar. He successfully demonstrated that they could soundly support the building.[2]

In a similar way, you can pressure test your brand pillars' ability to support your brand. First, see if they pass muster with your most experienced and insightful team members. Next, test them with your most critical customers to see if they believe your brand pillars are differentiating and relevant.

YOUR PILLARS BUILD ON YOUR PURPOSE AND SUPPORT YOUR PROMISE

Your brand pillars build on your brand purpose and support your brand promise. As in Greek architecture, think of your pillars as columns supporting the pediment or capstone promise of your brand

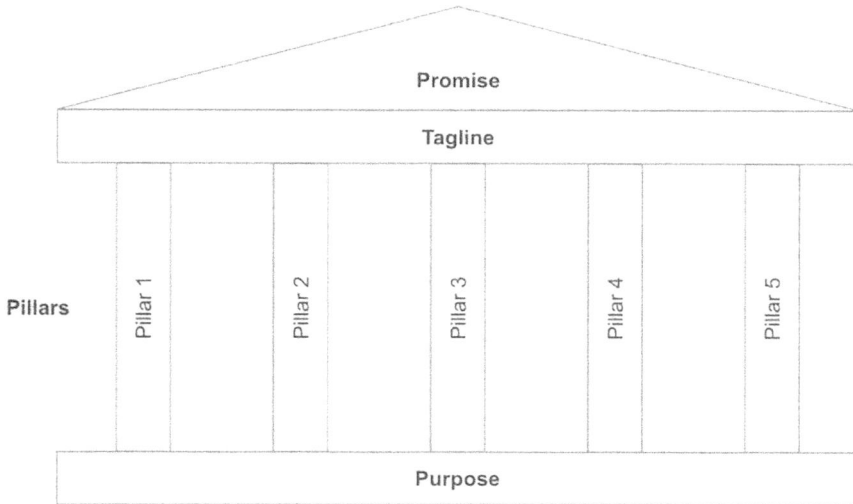

story structure. Each pillar is a load-bearing element in your story. They work together to sustain and uphold your story by delivering on your promise.

Removing a pillar would weaken your structure and compromise the integrity of your story. Each element of your Brand Foundation has an important role in creating a strong, differentiated, and lasting brand story.

Communicate Your Pillars

Founders and CEOs can often freestyle their way through new business meetings or high-ticket sales scenarios because they're good at thinking on their feet and can pivot on demand based on what customers say and do in the moment. However, banking on the superpowers of a few team members isn't a reliable way to scale your brand. To do that, you've got to equip *everyone* on your team with clear, concise talking points to communicate with your customers consistently throughout the different stages of their buying journeys.

First of all, your brand pillars should be concise. They should read as simple, straightforward sentences. If they wrap onto a second line, they're probably too long. You have to put in the work to distill complexity into simple summary statements that anyone on your team can speak with clarity, consistency, and confidence.

The less you say, the more they hear. You're not getting paid by the word, so keep it short and sweet. Brevity is best when it comes to communicating your message. Find a way to say it shorter. The goal is to articulate the quintessence of the thing, which Jerry Seinfeld defines as "something that is perfectly itself. You can't add or subtract anything to it without ruining it."[3]

Be sure to use conversational language in writing your brand pillars. They should be written in your brand voice, not marketing speak or acronym-laden alphabet soup. Try them out in conversations with your team and customers to see how they feel. You ought to be able to talk about your brand pillars naturally, flowingly, without straining to remember the right words. Of course, you'll want to internalize your brand pillars and commit them to memory without stressing too much about reciting them verbatim. Permit yourself to paraphrase them as long as you get the main ideas across without putting a premium on perfect recall.

Don't be afraid to shuffle the deck and change the order in which you present your pillars when needed. It's optimal to share them from greatest to least important, but changing up the sequence is okay, depending on your audience and the point of entry that makes the most sense for a given context or conversation. You'll want to be so familiar and comfortable with your pillars that you can share and teach them in whatever order makes sense for each situation.

Like an Olympic skier doing a gold-medal mogul run, pick your line down the mountain based on current conditions. Knowing the messages you want to convey in advance is like knowing the tricks you want to perform as you descend. Find the best spots to showcase your best messages as though you are popping your aerial tricks off the best bumps as you work your way downhill.

Remember to make your brand pillars all about your clients and the benefits they derive from your services and offerings. All they care about is "What's in it for me?" If you're not careful, you can accidentally flip the script and start talking about what you get from your brand pillars. You can avoid this frequent pitfall by reading your brand pillars out loud as a team and viewing them from a client's point of view. Better yet, you should test them with clients to ensure they're landing as intended and communicating the right ideas in the right ways.

The Body of Your Brand Narrative

Your five brand pillars form the outline and body of your brand narrative, which consists of your one-line elevator pitch, your one-paragraph about us statement, and your one-page company overview. The body of your narrative uses your brand pillars and benefits as section headings. It expands and extrapolates upon them in paragraph-long explanations of the reasons why they're important and how they make life better for your customers. These headlines and paragraphs become a reservoir to draw from when writing your website copy and other marketing communications.

A client of ours, Kinectify, is an anti-money-laundering (AML) risk management company. The founder and CEO of Kinectify, Joseph Martin, grew up in the AML industry professionally and could make a compelling case for Kinectify in one-on-one sales opportunities with prospective clients. As he built out his team, it became clear he needed to write down his story so others could learn and share it effectively. We worked with Joseph to build his brand story, including brand pillars that set his company apart, as outlined here. These pillars and their corresponding paragraphs became the basis for Kinectify's website copy, sales battle cards, trade show graphics, and marketing collateral.

1. Visibility: Continuously monitor your transaction activities in real time.

Through Kinectify's sophisticated AI-powered alerts engine, gaming companies can continuously monitor customer transaction activities in real time. Businesses can also reduce duplicate work and blind spots by understanding customers' transactions throughout their enterprises. In addition, the Kinectify platform empowers companies to efficiently conduct thorough risk assessments and gap analyses of their operations. Kinectify keeps them updated on changing AML laws and regulations locally, nationally, and globally. Kinectify also helps clients assess their organizational risk to identify and close any gaps.

2. Flexibility: Control every aspect of your AML programs.

With advanced configuration menus and a suite of features, Kinectify allows gaming companies to control every aspect of their AML programs. Users can set risk thresholds, create custom alerts, and configure monitoring standards. Organizations can also quickly adapt to changing regulatory requirements and market conditions and tailor their AML process to their unique preferences.

3. Scalability: Scale compliance efficiently.

Automating workflows is essential to scaling compliance efficiently. With Kinectify, clients can scale up their products and services while eliminating unnecessary software and reducing compliance friction. They can also seamlessly handle seasonal and transactional data surges.

4. Advisory: Scale your AML capacity up and down with ease.

Under the direction of AML industry experts, clients of Kinectify's advisory services can scale their capacity up and down with ease. The Kinectify Advisors team has extensive experience in gaming regulatory compliance. As a result, clients can tap into Kinectify's top AML talent on a fractional basis to meet their compliance deadlines and clear their backlogs.

5. Premier data partners: Access global data sets.

Kinectify works with premiere data partners, including Dow Jones and LexisNexis, to give clients access to global data sets on net worth, litigation, media, watchlists, and other critical KYC data.

- 6.3B+: Access to information from 6B people + 300M companies

- 60+: Global research capabilities in 60+ languages

- 250M: Net worth estimates on 40M people in U.S. and 250M people globally

- 160: Global watchlists

- 30K+: Screening information on professional athletes

Like Kinectify, you can leverage your investment by clearly stating your brand pillars across various communication touch points. When you know what to say, your communications are easier, more precise, and more consistent.

Your brand pillars can also help organize and prioritize your customer case studies. They provide a helpful filter for determining what stories matter most in showing customers what success looks like. Your pillars make it easier to recognize the case studies that would best encapsulate examples of the problems you solve and the outcomes customers realize when they put your five differentiators to work. In building out your library of customer case studies, always consider the customer segments and use cases that matter most to your business and brand pillars.

Pillars of Strength

Strong brand pillars provide the support you need to make your brand promise and story credible. The more highly differentiated and clear your brand pillars are, the better prepared you will be to explain what makes your business unique and why your audiences should care. One good way to think about pillars is to consider how communities sometimes honor people who embody the best among their citizens.

The regional chamber of commerce in my area recognizes individuals who exemplify the attributes of supporting the local economy and quality of life with a Pillar of the Valley award. The chamber hosts a gala dinner and program each year to reflect on award recipients' significant contributions. You can celebrate your differentiators similarly by recognizing the unique features and benefits that set your brand apart and by shining a spotlight on them.

CHAPTER 9

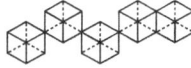

BRAND PERSONALITY

"The world will ask you who you are,
and if you don't know, the world will tell you."

—Carl Jung

On his long-running podcast, *Under the Influence*, host and veteran adman Terry O'Reilly says, "The task of advertising is really three-fold. First, it should create a distinct personality for the product in the marketplace. Second, it should highlight a unique benefit that separates the product from the competition. And lastly, it should send people to a location where that product can be purchased."[1] But before you can create effective advertising, you've got to define your brand's personality consistent with your brand strategy. Otherwise, you risk giving the wrong impression and detracting from your desired brand perception.

Creating a distinct personality for your brand starts by choosing modifiers (adjectives) that define your brand and can guide the ongoing creative efforts of everyone who's working on giving expression to your brand and bringing it to market—from your ads, content marketing, social media, and PR to your internal employee and investor communications. Nike's brand personality is athletic and heroic. Johnson & Johnson's is caring and compassionate. Harley-Davidson's is rowdy and rebellious. Each of these brand personalities is clear, consistent, and intentional. If you don't deliberately define what you want the personality of your brand to be, others may define it for you by filling the void with their ideas and potentially taking your brand down the wrong path.

Content creators, including creative directors, designers, writers, photographers, and videographers, can have competing views of your brand, creating inconsistencies, distractions, and disbelief among customers. Some creatives may bias your brand toward their personal preferences, misapply a playbook they borrowed from a previous experience, or manipulate your brand to feather their portfolio with an award-winning campaign that takes your brand down a dead end. Whatever the reason, if you don't provide your creative team with clearly defined brand personality guidelines, they may widen the gap between you and your customers instead of helping you close it.

A strategic, thoughtful, coordinated, and consistent approach to defining your brand personality and aligning everyone to it helps reinforce what your brand stands for in customers' minds. Each customer touch point, campaign, and creative contribution ought to reinforce your desired brand perception and enhance your brand equity with customers—like compounding interest—rather than allowing random weathervane acts of marketing to take your brand in whichever direction the wind blows.

Great organizations deliberately and systematically make moves toward a clearly defined branding goal. Like a sailboat navigator, they use any headwinds to their advantage by tacking into them and propelling themselves toward their goals instead of letting whoever happens to be at the helm steer their brand off course. As the captain of your ship, you need to chart a clearly defined course and hold your brand stewards accountable for driving toward it on each and every watch.

In some cases, brands have successfully collaborated with their audiences to cocreate and evolve their personality. The *Minions* movie franchise, produced by computer animation studio Illumination, allows and encourages fans to have fun with its characters by creating and sharing memes on social media and dressing up like the Minions at movie theaters. Of course, organic brand interpretations that make a bad impression can take your brand places you don't want it to go or create associations that are hard to recover from. Even beloved Minion pop culture suffered some blowback from kids begging their middle-aged moms to stop it already with mom memes paired with Minion images, like "If stress burned calories, I'd be a supermodel" and "'EXERCISE'? I thought you said, 'Extra Fries'!"

Hard versus Soft Differentiators

Ideally, companies strive to develop hard differentiators for their offerings—differentiators that set their brands apart based on real advantages and benefits—the things competitors can't match. However, if there aren't meaningful differences between your brand and your competitors, you can still set your brand apart based on soft differentiators, such as brand personality. How your brand looks, sounds, and feels can significantly impact how customers perceive its value and relevance in their lives, even if the performance between your brand and the alternatives isn't as differentiated as you might like.

For instance, Luxottica, a leading eyewear manufacturer, owns, makes, and markets multiple eyewear brands, like Oakley and Ray-Ban, that essentially have the same functional attributes and provide similar benefits. They differentiate themselves through dramatically different brand personalities. Customers identify with other brands within the Luxottica product portfolio based on how their reputations reflect on them and align with their sense of self.

The collective consciousness of popular culture influences much of this brand-matching process. How consumer brands, in particular, are woven into popular culture within a specific era or period determines their perceived value. Brands must continually calibrate themselves to the lens each new generation brings to the brand-consumer relationship or risk becoming irrelevant.

Archetypes

Speaking of the collective consciousness, Carl Jung, the famous Swiss psychiatrist who was a contemporary of Sigmund Freud and one of the founders of psychoanalysis, famously wrote about the collective unconscious, the genetically inherited, deepest part of our unconscious. According to Jung, our collective unconscious is where universal patterns and archetypes reside. Jung combined his theory of the unconscious with his study of religious and mythological symbolism, including folklore and legends from various cultures, and observed universally recurring patterns and motifs.

Jung's foundational work, or core archetypes and personas, evolved into twelve archetypes, each with its own personality or character traits. For years, brand strategists have used these archetypes to inform the brand personality definition and development process. Following are the names and descriptions of these archetypes along with an example of a well-known brand commonly associated with each of them:

The Innocent—Dove: Exhibits happiness, goodness, optimism, safety, and youth.

The Sage—National Geographic: Committed to helping the world gain deeper insight and wisdom, the Sage serves as the thoughtful mentor or advisor.

The Explorer—Jeep: Finds inspiration in travel, risk, discovery, and the thrill of new experiences.

The Outlaw—Harley-Davidson: Questions authority and breaks the rules; the Outlaw craves rebellion and revolution.

The Magician—Disney: Wishes to create something special and make dreams a reality; the Magician is a spiritual visionary.

The Hero—Nike: On a mission to make the world a better place, the Hero is courageous, bold, and inspirational.

The Lover—Chanel: Creates intimate moments and inspires love, passion, romance, and commitment.

The Jester—M&M's: Brings joy to the world through humor, fun, and irreverence and often likes to make some mischief.

The Everyman—Home Depot: Seeks connections and belonging; is recognized as supportive, faithful, and down to earth.

The Caregiver—Johnson & Johnson: Protects and cares for others; is compassionate, nurturing, and generous.

The Ruler—Rolex: Creates order from the chaos; the Ruler is typically controlling, stern, responsible, and organized.

The Artist—LEGO: Imaginative, inventive, and driven to build things of enduring meaning and value.[2]

Defining your brand's personality through the lens of brand archetypes can help you and your team consistently represent your brand creatively through all your brand communications. Remember that, like people, brands are multidimensional and blend more than one archetype. We typically advise clients to choose two or three brand archetypes, with one archetype playing the lead and one or two others serving in a supporting role. Different aspects of your brand's personality may play a more prominent role in your brand communications, depending on the customer context and stage within the customer journey.

By clearly defining your brand personality and consistently expressing it throughout all your brand communications, you help customers understand what you stand for and attract customers who share your values and brand sensibility—people who can relate to and see something of themselves in your brand. Remember, fully embracing a brand identity requires a deep commitment to showing up in the world in a way that reinforces your desired brand perception and sets you apart from the competition. When you're clear about your brand personality, consistently communicating it verbally, visually, and experientially becomes a lot easier for you and everyone on your team.

Creating Your Brand Identity: Visuals and Tone of Voice

The way your brand should look stems from the character of your brand as defined in the brand archetype matching process. Asking analogous questions can help uncover insights into your visual brand personality, such as, "If your brand were a car or truck, which one would it be and why?" If your customers think Land Rover is analogous to your brand, that suggests a very different set of personality traits than a Honda, a Jaguar, an Audi, a Tesla, or a 1968 Chevrolet pickup.

Using apparel brands can also work, assuming your interviewees are familiar enough with that product category to draw meaningful comparisons. For example, knowing your brand reminds your ideal customers of Lululemon and not Lands' End gives your brand permission to do and say certain things and to look a certain way. You can use almost any analogy if you and your customers relate to it and understand what it represents to your brand-building efforts.

Summarizing these traits involves choosing three or four adjectives to describe your brand visually. They must be observable aesthetic qualities to give your creative team meaningful direction; trios of modifiers like "industrial, urban, and modern" or "outdoor, Western, and rugged" work well—internal character traits like "courageous, competitive, and confident" do not because they aren't observable in the physical realm.

Besides providing direction for your visual brand communication, your brand personality informs your brand tone of voice: what your brand sounds like when spoken aloud or in the written word. Whereas marketing messages define *what* to say, brand tone of voice guidelines provide principles for *how* to say it, including something as simple as how your brand greets a prospective customer. Does your brand say, "Hey," "Hello," "Hi," or "Howdy"? Where does your brand sit on the formality continuum? What other themes define your brand voice, and how does your brand operate within them?

HUMOR				
Serious				Funny
FORMALITY				
Casual				Formal
RESPECT				
Sassy				Respectful
ENTHUSIASM				
Matter-of-Fact				Enthusiastic

(Source: Ebaqdesign, "7 Best Examples of Brand Voice & Tone," https://www.ebaqdesign.com/blog/brand-voice.)

Determining the ideal personality for your brand starts with a clear understanding of who your ideal customers are, how they view the world, and how they see your brand fitting into their values and lifestyles. Focusing on creating the correct customer perception of your brand will help you avoid the classic pitfall of basing your brand's personality on the personality of your founder or leaders. While founders' values often and rightfully inform the company's values and shape its culture, the personality of your brand ought to reflect the wants and values of your customers, not those of the people who run your business. Taking this approach is a freeing concept since the products and services you offer may not be something the leaders of your business consume, want, or need. Forcing your brand's personality to reflect the personality of your leaders or employees is an arbitrary and unnecessary limiting factor. If they happen to align, great, but don't insist on it. Focus instead on creating a brand personality that resonates with your customers.

Once you've established parameters for your brand personality, it's vital you consistently apply and implement them. If not, you can cause confusion by leaving the door open for interpretations that lead your brand astray. In practical terms, you're trying to suspend disbelief that your brand is anything other than what you say it is. To build strong belief in your brand, you've got to consistently apply your brand personality guidelines across all your customer touch points. Any gaps or inconsistencies in execution can break the spell and cast seeds of doubt in your customers' and employees' hearts and minds.

Branding aims to create an emotional connection between your brand and the people who buy your products and services, a connection that transcends transactions and helps form lasting, loyal relationships. One way of achieving this goal from a brand personality standpoint is to consider creating a mascot that helps humanize your brand and communicates a relatable personality, if only metaphorically.

BambooHR developed a friendly-looking panda mascot that embodies its founders' cheery, outgoing personalities and aligns with the kinder, gentler HR community BambooHR serves.

Tanner, the accounting and advisory firm for whom we did a brand refresh, wanted to position itself as the premier independent accounting and advisory firm in its market. Our design partner, Bill Chiaravalle, designed an owl icon to visually express Tanner's brand strategy and quickly communicate Tanner's wisdom to its clients. Culturally speaking, going as far back as the Greek goddess Athena, owls represent wisdom; they sit on your shoulder and help you see your blind spots. Stage blindness is an inevitable problem for the founders of successful startups as they move from one stage of growth to another and face new challenges and levels of complexity they've never encountered. They don't know what they don't know, but Tanner does—using an owl as Tanner's icon reinforces its sage-advisor personality in helping startups grow and prepare for liquidity events. Tanner provides growth companies with the right answers to move forward with clarity and confidence and maximize the valuations of their companies when it's the right time to sell.

The strategies for these two brand personalities are similar but brand specific, meaning they aren't interchangeable. Whereas a friendly panda feels appropriate for BambooHR and its people-driven HR customers and community, Tanner's clients would have seen a panda logo as too silly and not credible for a numbers-driven accounting and advisory firm. Despite Tanner's owl logo feeling appropriate for Tanner's wisdom-oriented brand positioning and narrative, it would have come across as being too aloof for BambooHR—not to mention a panda fits nicely with BambooHR's name.

With a name like BambooHR and a panda brand mascot, it would have been easy for the company to lean into additional Asian references and design motifs. However, the founders wanted to shine a spotlight on the essence of their brand story, which revolved around enabling HR professionals to focus on helping people rather than on paperwork. They provided clear guidelines and parameters to not let the personality of the brand overshadow or detract from its brand positioning or narrative or get too far afield from its core purpose of setting people free to do great work. With this goal in mind, the founders determined early on, for example, that pagodas were too distracting for BambooHR's brand imagery and kept visual references to bamboo at a minimum.

Another critical input in building a successful brand personality is knowing where your brand will land along the mass-market-to-premium continuum. Something as simple as incorporating black into your brand color palette or employing white space in your visual brand communications can take the perception of your brand upmarket. Skillful designers and writers know how to elevate a brand by making subtle yet significant choices to achieve the appropriate degree of formality or informality in their creative expressions of a brand.

One exercise we've employed to help clients clearly define their brand personality is to ask them and their customers to imagine the brand is knocking at their door. In their mind's eye, who do they see standing there when they open it? We facilitate a conversation about what makes that individual representative of the brand: What were they wearing, saying, and doing? From there, we infer human personality traits and translate them into defining brand personality traits.

Make Believe

Defining and consistently living a unique and appropriate brand personality builds belief in your brand for customers. It's crucial to be consistent with your brand personality because the objective of branding, after all, is the process of persuading your customers to believe in your brand. Building belief in your brand is a world-making process where your brand personality is complete, congruent, and consistent.

A friend of mine worked for a packaging design agency that did projects for General Mills. One time, they were presenting some design concepts for Lucky Charms, the cereal brand, to the client team, and one of the design concepts included an image of Lucky the Leprechaun wearing a watch. The client quickly corrected the agency, saying it was inappropriate for Lucky to wear a watch because "there is no time where Lucky lives." Including a watch for Lucky was out of character for the make-believe—but consistent and intentional—world General Mills had created for the character of the Lucky brand. Similarly, anyone building a brand takes on a world-making initiative that requires thoughtful consideration of what is and isn't acceptable, appropriate, or congruent with the rules of engagement for that world. Defining a clear, consistent brand personality is foundational to the world-making process.

In the classic love story and movie *Somewhere in Time*, Christopher Reeve's character, Richard Collier, falls in love with a woman (Elise McKenna, played by Jane Seymour) in a vintage photograph at the hotel where he's staying. Richard becomes so mesmerized by Elise that he learns everything he can about her and seeks the guidance of a time traveler who teaches him how to convince himself he's back in time.

Richard dresses in period clothing to make himself believe in his temporal fluidity. He repeats the same mantra over and over to himself, suggesting the year is 1912, and eventually finds himself transported back in time, where he woos and wins the heart of his love interest. Together, they overcome various obstacles and are in the bliss of their love match when Richard innocently pulls a penny out of his pants trousers only to discover—to his shock and dismay—that it's dated 1982. The penny moment breaks the spell and takes him back to his hotel room instantly, where he finds himself alone and heartbroken.

If we're not careful in managing our brands to have a consistent and cohesive brand personality, we can create similar penny moments that introduce dissonance and disbelief in the minds of our customers, giving them reason to question who we are or if we can truly deliver on the promises we've made. When our brands stay in character and present themselves in alignment with our desired identity, we build trust and confidence in our customers and can create strong relationships with them.

PHASE 3

BRAND EXPRESSION

"I want freedom for the full expression of my personality."

—Mahatma Gandhi

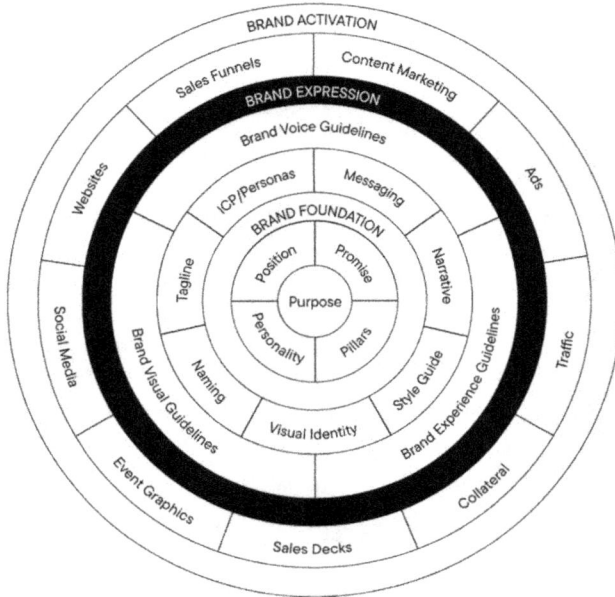

The third phase of The Backstory Brand Wheel Framework is about defining the words, images, and experiences that will shape and influence how customers see and value your brand—your brand perception. To reiterate, the foundation of creating a successful brand strategy is knowing who your audiences are, what they want, and what's in their way from the viewpoint of your brand being able to address those unmet needs. These insights form a filter, telling you and your team what to invite into your brand world and what to keep out.

Successful brands have a clear sense of purpose and identity; this clarity helps them avoid following temporary trends, falling into the trap of imitating other brands, or trying to be better than a competitor at what they do best. Instead, brand leaders focus on doing different things and doing things differently, which is the essence of strategy. They zig when others zag, creating a clear sense of separation and differentiation, giving customers a choice that better aligns with their attitudes, beliefs, and values and creates a more meaningful and lasting brand connection. Done well, this clarity of choice commands a premium as well as advocacy among true believers and followers who align with your brand and make it a winner.

In working with Bacon, the on-demand temp work app, the founder and CEO of the company, Hunter Sebresos, shared his transformative story with us, from a latchkey kid with a competitive chip on his shoulder to a highly effective creative director turned business designer and leader. In listening to him, we heard a throughline epitomizing Hunter's growth mindset and Bacon's best employers and workers. Bacon's "Hustle and Shine" brand mantra encapsulates Hunter's grit and determination to follow in the footsteps of his hardworking single mom and his willingness to accept and act on the guidance and direction of a high school teacher who recognized Hunter's innate creative abilities.

At the pivotal age of sixteen, Hunter shifted from being a venting victim to becoming a bold free agent who chose to make the most of his opportunities. Step by step, Hunter made good on his commitments:

- Graduating from high school with a growing interest in art

- Serving in the Marines as a tank commander

- Serving a church mission in the Philippines

- Winning a coveted advertising internship in New York as an undergraduate college student

- Getting married and becoming a dependable husband and father

- Working at the NASA Jet Propulsion Laboratory (JPL) in Pasadena while earning an MFA at ArtCenter College of Design

- Moving his family to Kenya to learn how to design and operate successful micro franchises that solved problems for local communities and created jobs for the people who lived there

- Pivoting from the VP of marketing for a failed startup to conceiving and executing Bacon's effective business model as its founder and CEO

Hunter built Bacon to give single moms and dads—and underdogs everywhere—the opportunity to level up their lives with a bit of hustle. Today, thousands of people are shifting to purposeful temp work that allows them to gain crucial personal success skills while paying the bills, skills they need for long-term career success. From a Brand Expression standpoint, Bacon's collective "Hustle and Shine" mindset informs every aspect of the brand's tone of voice and visual brand identity.

Hunter grew up wearing a black bomber jacket and continues to embrace this street-smart look as a visual metaphor for people making the most of the Bacon platform and the opportunities it affords them to move from shift workers to career-minded professionals. And he doesn't just wear the jacket, he gives one to new employees as a tangible reminder of Bacon's "Do the work" ethos, which has fueled his career and the company's growth.

Our in-depth interviews as part of our engagement with Bacon confirmed and validated that the founding members of the Bacon team as well as standout customers and employer partners share Hunter's values. Bacon's brand purpose statement is "To show the world what a little hustle can do," and the audience-specific messaging framework we collaboratively designed with Hunter and his team builds upon this foundational idea.

Staying true to your purpose through all your brand expressions will help you make decisions that align with your core brand values and communicate them in an authentic way that resonates with employees, customers, and partners who share your values. In the following three chapters, you will learn how to create guidelines for expressing your brand verbally, visually, and experientially. These principles will help ensure your entire team aligns around communicating your brand in a way that sets it apart and continually reminds them of what your brand stands for in the process.

CHAPTER 10

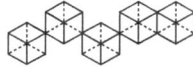

MARKETING MESSAGING

"What is your Unique Selling Proposition?
What makes you different than your competitors?
Wrap your advertising message around that USP and
communicate it in a clear and concise manner."

—Lynda Resnick

Resonating with your customers is the ultimate desired outcome of effective marketing messaging. Resonance results from solving a significant customer problem and communicating your solution's features, advantages, and benefits so customers recognize they can't afford not to change what they're doing and how they're doing it. When many customers realize the pain of staying the same is greater than the pain of making the change with the help of your products and services, you've found a growth market.

Creating resonant marketing messages starts with an in-depth understanding of who your audiences are, what they want, and the problems that stand in their way of getting it—issues your solution is uniquely qualified to resolve for them. This understanding informs the development of clear, consistent messages that communicate the features, advantages, benefits—and outcomes—of your offerings.

You can't create clear, consistent messaging that communicates the problem-solving capabilities of your solutions until you have validated your business model and achieved product-market fit. Once you've completed these fundamental steps, you can use our Message Market Fit process to iteratively test and refine marketing messages and find the ones that resonate with your customers. The underlying principles driving this iterative process apply to established companies and start-ups bringing new products and services to market.

Business Model Validation

The Lean Canvas is a one-page business plan template Ash Maurya adapted for startups based on Alex Osterwalder's Business Model Canvas. In addition to the Lean Canvas, Maurya is the creator of the LEANSTACK continuous innovation funnel and the author of *Running Lean*. Using Lean Canvas, you can iteratively test and refine your assumptions about your business model and, building on this base, find product-market fit.

Maurya's template includes a step for a unique value proposition, defined as "a single, clear, compelling value proposition that turns an unaware visitor into an interested prospect."[1] We refer to this over-arching value proposition or message as your *brand promise*. It's an essential aspect of your messaging strategy, but it's just the beginning. In addition to a brand promise, you must clarify and articulate supporting value propositions or messages that are audience- and offering-agnostic, along with value propositions specific to each of your audiences and products.

Problem List your customers' top 3 problems	Solution Outline possible solutions for each problem	Unique value proposition Singular, clear, compelling statement that turns an unaware visitor into an interested prospect	Unfair advantage Something that can't be easily copied or bought	Customer segments List your target customers and users
Existing alternatives List how these problems are solved today	Key metrics List key numbers telling how your business is doing today	High-level concept List your X for Y analogy (e.g., YouTube = Flickr for videos)	Channels List your paths to customers	Early adopters List characteristics of your ideal customer
Cost structure List your fixed and variable costs		Revenue streams List your sources of revenue		

Lean Canvas is adapted from Business Model Canvas and is licensed under the Creative Commons Attributions-Share Alike 3.0 Un-ported License.

(Source: LEANFoundry, Lean Canvas,
https://www.leanfoundry.com/tools/lean-canvas.)

Articulating and validating your unique value proposition is essential to building an effective business model. It will be evident you've done your homework by iteratively testing and refining your marketing messages as the result will be sales traction that generates actual revenue. Traction wins the respect of partners and investors who take an evidence-based approach to aligning themselves with new and growing businesses that have moved beyond proof of concept.

When you discover and articulate a differentiating brand promise, consider its significant implications for your business model and operations. Finding words that resonate is just half the solution; you and your team must also ensure that your organization and operations can fulfill your brand promise. Take the time you need to get your operational house in order so your organization can live up to your promise day in and day out before taking it to market. Making a promise you can't keep is like writing checks your organization can't cash; bouncing checks in this way breaks trust and leaves your employee and customer relationships worse off than if you'd never made the promise in the first place.

Product-Market Fit

Andy Rachleff, the cofounder of Wealthfront and Benchmark Capital, is credited with developing the idea of product-market fit. He stated:

> Identifying a compelling value hypothesis is what I call finding product-market fit. A value hypothesis addresses both the features and business model required to entice a customer to buy your product. Companies often go through many iterations before they find product-market fit, if they ever do.
>
> Steve [Blank] and Eric [Ries] recommend that entrepreneurs first nail their value hypothesis before tackling their growth hypothesis. After all, if the dogs don't want to eat the dog food then what good is attracting a lot of dogs? You can waste a lot of money if you don't follow their prescribed order, because you'll spend more money on growth than determining value.[2]

Those crucial pieces show you how your offering fits—or doesn't—and allows you to adjust as needed. Ash Maurya says, "Most startups fail not because we fail to build what we set out to build but because we fail to find the right customers, the right markets for our products. You have to build a great product, but you have to make the rest of the Business Model Canvas work as well. You have to get these pieces to fit together like you would fit a jigsaw puzzle."[3] He suggests using three to five actionable conversion metrics to achieve product-market fit, which he adopted from Dave McClure:

1. **Acquisition:** How do users find you?

2. **Activation:** Do users have a great first experience with your product?

3. **Retention:** Do users come back and use your product?

4. **Referral:** Do users tell others about your product?

5. **Revenue:** How do you make money?

Maurya further clarifies this process by saying, "It's important to frame the metrics as specific actions the user takes which makes them both measurable and actionable."[4] And his book, *Running Lean*, dedicates fifty pages to this topic.

Message Market Fit

Our Message Market Fit process applies the iterative build-measure-learn principles of product-market fit to the development of clear, concise, and consistent marketing messages that resonate with customers. Learning how to achieve Message Market Fit is essential for building a brand that scales—especially for matrixed multi-audience, multi-offering messaging frameworks. In our experience, companies can have valid business models and may have achieved product-market fit, but if their sales funnels are small and slow, they may lack Message Market Fit. Until they resolve this issue, they can't scale significantly or profitably. Our Message Market Fit process helps businesses and organizations systematically create effective messaging to accelerate profitable growth.

Creating and validating compelling messaging starts with designing messaging prototypes. As shown in the messaging concept framework that follows, a messaging concept has five elements: audience, pain point, solution, benefit, and reason to believe. Each component builds on the last to create a message that resonates with customers, persuading them to engage with you and learn more about your offering and how it can help them solve their problems. Once you have built a working set of messaging prototypes, you measure their effectiveness through customer interviews and feedback.

During our Message Market Fit process, you create and test multiple options of the problem, solution, benefit, and reason to believe sections to find out which versions of each element of the concept resonate with customers and why or why not. Testing these options also indicates which of these to prioritize if more than one resonates within each section.

MESSAGING CONCEPT FRAMEWORK	
Audience	The name of the audience and a brief description of them
Problem	A problem statement from the customer's perspective
Solution	A brief description of your product or service
Benefit	The benefit a customer receives from your offering
Reason to Believe	A proof point that instills confidence in your solution and benefit

AUDIENCE

Defining your audience is the first element within the messaging concept framework. It will include the name of the audience and a brief description of who they are, as well as psychographic and demographic information, with the emphasis on psychographics to describe an audience's psychological or qualitative attributes, such as attitudes, values, beliefs, and behaviors. In contrast, demographics focus on quantitative characteristics, such as gender, age, education level, household income, and location. Psychographics offer a richer and more meaningful source of brand marketing insights than demographics in helping you effectively find and connect with your audience.

You can get this audience information from your Ideal Customer Profiles (ICP) and customer persona, or "avatar," descriptions for each audience or customer segment. However, an abbreviated version of the ICP is usually best, given the limited space of a messaging concept.

PROBLEM STATEMENTS

Write problem statements in first person to reflect your deep understanding and empathy for what an audience wants and what's in their way of getting it. Problem statements should highlight the problems your offerings can uniquely solve, or there is no point in writing them. Base them on fundamental insights from customer observations and conversations—not assumptions, generalizations, or stereotypes.

Debating what your customers want among your internal team is unproductive. Internal debates tend to favor the most influential person or most prominent voice in the room, however uninformed they may be. If you're unsure of what your audience wants, openly admit it, fill out this section with your best guesses, and then test and refine them based on real customer feedback until your audience confirms you have a correct understanding of their pain points and have articulated them in a way that resonates.

SOLUTION STATEMENTS

Write solution statements in second person to name and describe your offerings, including their key features and advantages—what they do and how they work. Solution statements should highlight the most compelling aspects of your offering for the specific audience of each messaging concept. Again, the beauty of the build-measure-learn approach to our Message Market Fit process is you don't have to endlessly debate whose opinion is correct about which words will resonate with customers. The product-market fit process popularized by Eric Ries in *The Lean Startup* identifies what customers want in a product and the channels used to deliver it by testing and refining early product hypotheses and assumptions. However, the Message Market Fit process tests and refines messaging concepts until customers confirm you've reached resonance with them.

BENEFIT STATEMENTS

Write declarative benefit statements in the imperative mood and keep them succinct. Remember, they should speak to a specific audience and the corresponding problem statement within their messaging concept. In contrast, general benefits fall under your brand or company messaging.

Keep your benefits brief so they fit on one line. If they wrap onto a second line, reduce them to their essence. Remember, a well-crafted benefit statement can function as a headline, which typically has seven words or less. Like reading the headline of a billboard while flying down the freeway, your benefit statements only have a few seconds to make a good first impression when a potential customer scans your website, social post, trade show booth, or ad. If your headlines are too long, they won't work.

REASONS TO BELIEVE

Reasons to believe give customers confidence that your offering can deliver on its promised benefit for them. What makes a reason to believe (RTB) effective can vary depending on your product category. "Nine out of ten dentists recommend Crest," but what about the ones who don't? Understanding what they recommend and why could open up a whole new category of toothpaste that, for the right audience, is the perfect fit with its own set of compelling reasons to believe.

For a SaaS product, a compelling reason to believe might be a short time to value—the time it takes for a customer to realize the value of your product from the time they purchase it. For a professional services firm, it might be a professional credential, your roster of current customers, or the longer-than-average tenure of your client relationships. For a commercial construction company, it might be the percentage of projects done on time and under budget. As with the other elements of your messaging concept, your reasons to believe should be as direct and to the point as possible. In addition to written reasons, be sure to keep in mind the customer's experience in using your products and services. The way you creatively convey experiential cues can significantly impact customers' perceptions of the value and believability of your offering.

Minimum Viable Messages and Iteration

The first version of your messaging concept is your minimum viable message (MVM). Like a minimum viable product (MVP), a minimum viable message is a prototype of a message you think will resonate with your customers but haven't tested yet. It represents your team's collective ideas about a value proposition or benefit statement that you believe will resonate with one of your audiences based on who they are, what they want, and what's in their way. Minimum viable messages get you started on the messaging development path, but they're just the beginning.

We typically include up to four MVM options within each section of a messaging concept—aside from the audience section, which has just one entry.

MESSAGING CONCEPT FRAMEWORK	
Audience	The name of the audience and a brief description of them
Problem	A problem statement from the customer's perspective A problem statement from the customer's perspective A problem statement from the customer's perspective A problem statement from the customer's perspective
Solution	A brief description of your product or service A brief description of your product or service A brief description of your product or service A brief description of your product or service
Benefit	The benefit a customer receives from your offering The benefit a customer receives from your offering The benefit a customer receives from your offering The benefit a customer receives from your offering
Reason to Believe	A proof point that instills confidence in your solution and benefit A proof point that instills confidence in your solution and benefit A proof point that instills confidence in your solution and benefit A proof point that instills confidence in your solution and benefit

Refining your MVM involves asking customers which options are most relevant within each section of your messaging concept and inviting them to change or eliminate any wording to better reflect their feelings and needs. After deleting irrelevant options, you reorganize the remaining options from most to least important according to your customers' preferences and priorities. This prioritization process is much easier once you know the message elements that resonate with your audiences and why.

You should develop a unique messaging concept for each audience to gather specific insights into each customer segment. After talking with three or more customers from each audience, you will start to see patterns and eventually reach a saturation point where you consistently get positive feedback on your refined messages. That's when you'll know you have a valid message to take to market.

If a message isn't resonating with a given audience, you either have the wrong messaging or the wrong audience. To find resonance, you'll need to pivot and change your audience or message—or both—until they align.

Remember, the goal is to communicate a compelling enough value proposition for your audience so they're genuinely motivated to buy your product or service. The messaging development process depends on meaningful MVM conversations with customers representing the right market segments. That's why being selective in who you invite to evaluate and provide feedback on your MVM is so important.

Using generic AI tools to generate marketing messages from scratch runs the risk of producing me-too value propositions derived from existing messages others are already using. To differentiate your messaging and narrative, you must go to the source by talking with customers and generating human-centered insights with an in-depth understanding of what customers want and why. The need to create distinctive messages based on unique insights is especially true for new products and services that offer something different and uniquely relevant. It applies to established categories too.

AI can be useful for synthesizing, formulating, or wordsmithing ideas that come from customers. It can also consolidate disparate inputs in aggregate for you to refine further as you create your custom message library.

Category messaging includes generalized value propositions any player in a given industry or product category can credibly claim as their own. Category messages represent high-level benefits that don't set your organization or offering apart. Separating your brand from the competition requires deeper insight and understanding than the prevailing wisdom and best practices already defined by established players, not simply repackaging it.

And, of course, pay-per-click advertising is another way to automate part of the messaging development process. AI can help you quickly generate messaging variations to evaluate through A/B testing. However, even A/B testing has limitations. While it can tell you which messages perform the best, it can't tell you why. It can't give you insights into the psychographics of the people who are clicking and converting, why specific messages resonate with them while others do not, or which parts of the messaging stand out and for what reasons.

Not knowing the answers to these foundational questions inhibits your ability to understand what to emphasize in your messaging. It makes it more difficult to create additional relevant messages and build narrative themes that attract the right audiences. For these reasons, we recommend using a qualitative approach to develop and test your messaging and then using A/B testing to fine-tune your messaging with quantitative feedback supported by analytics. Taking this dual qualitative-quantitative approach gives you the best of both worlds.

Your Messaging Framework

A messaging framework is a structured repository of marketing messages that clearly defines your audiences and articulates the problems you solve for them. It connects the features of your offerings—whether products, services, or solutions—to the advantages they provide, and ultimately to the benefits and outcomes your audiences care about most. An effective messaging framework becomes the single source of truth for your marketing, sales, customer success, product management, and product marketing teams—ensuring everyone is aligned and speaking the same language.

These frameworks help create internal alignment as well as a consistent experience for customers from the first step of their journey, when they realize they have a problem they can't afford not to solve, to learning about the criteria for solving it (your authoritative criteria). Ultimately, effective messaging concepts lead customers to your offering, the solution that satisfies and solves their problem, resulting in more revenue and profitable growth for your business.

Quality marketing messages elevate every aspect of your marketing and make a big impact on your marketing ROI and business outcomes. If your marketing messages are merely based on assumptions, anecdotes, uninformed opinions, or best guesses, they put your ability to connect with customers at risk. Effective messaging resonates with customers and speaks their language. The goal in building a comprehensive marketing messaging framework is gathering the best and most effective messaging in one location so everyone on your team can use it to stay on message all the time.

You should test and validate your marketing messages to maximize the ROI of your messaging framework. Messaging data can come from various sources ranging from qualitative conversations with customers at the point of sale, customer support calls, and in-depth interviews or surveys to marketing analytics and A/B tests. Whatever methods you use to inform and validate your marketing messages, the more actionable your insights are as to what's working and why, the stronger your marketing strategy. As a result, you and your teams will feel more confident, and your marketing will become more effective.

The investment of time, energy, and resources required to build an effective marketing messaging framework depends on the number of audiences and offerings you have. For simple brands serving one or two audiences with one or two products, articulating value propositions or marketing messages is relatively straightforward. For multi-product, multi-audience brands, the messaging development and validation process can be much more involved. Large marketing matrixes require more insights from more customers, as well as more time to analyze, synthesize, and distill messaging data into clearly distinctive and differentiated messages. It also requires collaborative input from a variety of team members who know each audience and product and have unique perspectives to contribute. The more complex the messaging framework, the greater the need to systematically define it.

As outlined in The Backstory Messaging Matrix that follows, robust, comprehensive, and flexible messaging strategies include four types of messages: (1) brand or company messaging, (2) audience messaging, (3) offering messaging, and (4) audience- and offering-specific messaging.

The Backstory Messaging Matrix

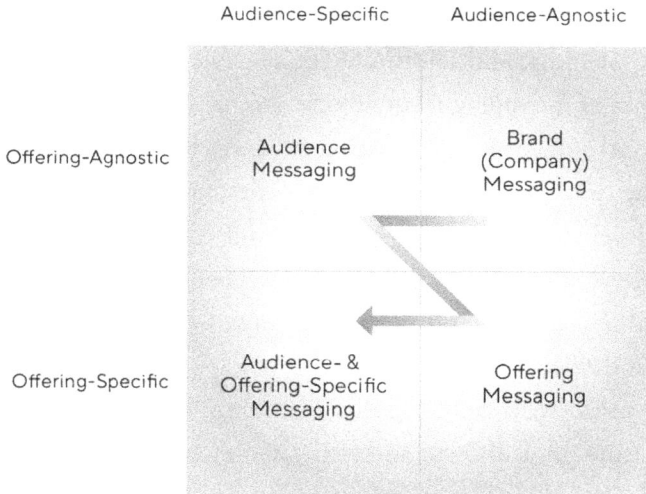

	Audience-Specific	Audience-Agnostic
Offering-Agnostic	Audience Messaging	Brand (Company) Messaging
Offering-Specific	Audience- & Offering-Specific Messaging	Offering Messaging

BRAND MESSAGING

Brand messaging, also known as company or umbrella messaging, articulates the types of problems your company solves—and the benefits you provide—for all your audiences. By definition, brand messaging is broad horizontal messaging relevant to all the types of companies and audiences you serve regardless of their industry, functional area, or department. Imagine giving a keynote address at a customer conference and having all your customers listen and resonate with your presentation simultaneously in the same room. Brand messaging serves this purpose. It aims to persuade prospective and existing customers to engage with you and want to learn more about how you can solve their problems with the benefits your offerings provide.

In contrast, audience and offering messaging are like the breakout sessions following the keynote address at a conference. Breakout sessions address specific topics, needs, questions, problems, pain points, use cases, jobs to be done, and solutions. The previous diagram shows how the four types of messaging relate to one another.

When all your audiences are listening to and reading the same words at the same time, you'll naturally need to elevate what you say to a more general level so everyone can relate to your messages. Getting too specific too soon risks deeply engaging some people while turning others off. For this reason, brand messaging must be inclusive of all your audiences and offerings.

In a perfect world, you would ideally communicate with each of your audiences through a discrete and dedicated channel—or, better yet, one-on-one—but that's not always possible or profitable, particularly if you serve multiple audiences with multiple offerings. When you don't yet know which segments prospective customers belong to, and they're at the top of the marketing funnel, you have to connect with them at a high level with generally relevant messages so they'll want to learn more, engage with your team, share more about themselves, and allow you to talk to them in context of their specific problems and use cases. Sharing increasingly relevant messages as customers progress on their buyer's journey through your funnel puts your brand on the shortlist of contenders for winning their business.

AUDIENCE MESSAGING

Unlike brand messaging, which talks to all your audiences at a high level, audience messaging addresses the particular concerns and questions of a specific audience or customer segment. Keep in mind that at this stage, you still aren't getting into the details of *how* you solve these problems (by delineating product features and advantages); that step comes next.

The more audiences your business and brand serve, the more challenging it is to develop and build a comprehensive messaging framework that clarifies and articulates targeted, audience-specific messages. Building a messaging framework is a time-intensive process requiring customer insights, experience, skill, and collaboration. In addition, it invites input from all your subject-matter experts to help you uncover, understand, and articulate the reasons different customers buy based on their unique pain points, use cases, and jobs to be done.

OFFERING MESSAGING

Offering messaging[5] describes your offering's general benefits and features independent of any one audience. A product feature names a specific characteristic, attribute, or function of an offering. A single feature or feature set (topic) can enable one or more advantages that result in one or more benefits. An advantage describes what a feature does or how it works. A benefit demonstrates how a feature makes life better for a customer. The cascading effect of these elements working together can create a growing number of messages the further you go downstream in your messaging hierarchy.

Developing offering messaging in a thoughtful, thorough way sets your team up for success, equipping them with the messaging they need to create compelling product marketing content and campaigns that progress customers through the middle of your marketing funnel. Offering messaging is essential in defining the criteria for your customers' success within your category. As discussed earlier, representing the five factors for success on your terms means customers are more likely to use *your* success criteria while shopping for and evaluating viable offerings to solve their problems.

AUDIENCE- AND OFFERING-SPECIFIC MESSAGING

The bottom of your marketing funnel contains audience- and offering-specific messaging as the final step in delivering a marketing-qualified lead to your sales team, vetted as being worthy of their valuable time and attention. This type of messaging is the most specific within the Messaging Funnel as it confirms how a particular product's features, advantages, and benefits address a specific audience's pain points. Think of audience- and offering-specific messaging as vertical messaging designed for a specific audience within a company or industry, in contrast to high-level horizontal brand messaging.

Building Out Your Messaging Framework

Building out each type of messaging is a systematic, repeatable process that requires a comprehensive framework, including messaging inputs and outputs. For B2B brands, messaging inputs begin with defining the firmographics of your ICPs, including company size, industry, product focus, number of employees, amount of revenue, sales channels, etc. From there, you define the characteristics of your customer personas, the individuals who make or influence buying decisions on behalf of their organizations. For clarification, B2B brands—businesses that sell to other businesses—have ICPs while B2C brands do not. The larger the company and size of the contract, the more people will be involved in the buying process. Buying committees or groups can have as many as five to eight participants—each representing a different customer persona—depending on the cost, complexity, and potential impact of a solution on an organization.

B2B MESSAGING FRAMEWORKS

In the B2B messaging framework example that follows, I've included a basic set of three personas, including the economic buyer, the person with the budget and authority to make the buying decision; the technical buyer, the individual who vets potential solutions from a technical performance, compatibility, and security standpoint; and the influencer, someone who influences a buying decision but doesn't have the authority to make the final decision. I've also included the user because including their information helps provide additional context for your overall value proposition. Users are the people who use your product or service even though they may not have a say in selecting it.

Rather than giving a customer persona a clever name, like "Law Firm Larry," I've found it works better to provide personas with easy-to-remember descriptive names combined with the names of real customers who are familiar to people within your team and are representative of your best audiences in terms of who they are, what they want, and what's in their way.

Step 1: Define Your Audiences

Name of ICP				
Firmographics				
Customer Personas	Economic Buyer	Technical Buyer	Influencer	User
Persona name				
Who they are				
What they want				
What's in their way				
Persona examples				

Step 2: Build Your Value Chain

The next step is to clarify and articulate the value you provide each audience with your offerings in a logical sequence. List the name of the audience in the first column and build out one row of information at a time. The information should include the name of each audience (ICP and/or customer persona), a first-person pain point or problem statement for them, and a corresponding offering, feature, advantage, and benefit specific to the audience and problem.

Audience	Pain Point	Offering	Feature	Advantage	Benefit

Remember to be descriptive in naming your customer personas. The name of each customer persona should immediately communicate who belongs to the audience for everyone on your team, including full-time employees, freelancers, and agencies. Keep problem statements singular, focused, brief, and to the point. Remember, a product feature names a specific product characteristic, attribute, or function. An advantage describes what a feature does or how it works.

A benefit articulates how a feature makes life better for a customer/consumer. It's important to distinguish between functional and emotional benefits. Functional benefits speak to the quality, functionality, or performance of a solution. Emotional benefits communicate the way using your products or services makes customers feel. A well-rounded messaging framework needs both functional and emotional benefits.

We refer to a complete row of information in a messaging framework as a value chain because it links all of the elements of a value proposition together for a specific audience and an unmet need. It's important to note that a single offering (product or service) may have multiple value chains and one feature may have more than one advantage and benefit. Even so, there should be just one benefit per value chain in your messaging framework to keep your messages clear and organized.

Defining useful value chains is a collaborative process drawing from the insights and observations of your product, marketing, sales, and client success teams. Creating a unified messaging framework strengthens and aligns working relationships among these groups. Participants build a better rapport and appreciation for one another and a shared understanding of how their company's offerings uniquely solve customers' problems. They're able to articulate the value of your offerings more clearly, consistently, and effectively. They tend to achieve greater success by working together to solve problems and pursue opportunities from the same side of the table instead of seeing one another as adversaries.

B2C MESSAGING FRAMEWORKS

The messaging inputs for B2C brands include defining your customer personas, including those who buy your products, those who influence buyers, and those who use your products. As with B2B brands, I recommend avoiding giving B2C customer personas clever names like "Sally Soccer Mom." From experience, it's better to use descriptive names combined with specific examples of customers who embody each persona.

Step 1: Define Your Audiences

Customer Personas	Buyer	Influencer	User
Persona name			
Who they are			
What they want			
What's in their way			
Persona examples			

Step 2: Articulate Your Value

The process of articulating the value a brand provides for B2C customers is very similar to the B2B approach described earlier. It follows the same steps and sequencing but without an ICP in the audience column since B2C brands sell directly to end consumers.

UNPACK ALL THE VALUE YOU CAN

Remember to unpack all the pain points, features, advantages, and benefits for your audiences open-endedly rather than capping them or putting an arbitrary limit on them. You can summarize the most important benefits as part of the message map development process for short content and campaign expressions of your value. However, you'll be glad you exhausted all the ideas for marketing messages when it comes to maintaining a steady content publishing cadence as part of your ongoing content marketing strategy.

Google and other search engines reward brands that provide helpful information with higher search rankings. We're talking about link-worthy content other sites reference in their articles and posts that boost your online credibility and authority. Supplying a steady stream of relevant content can be exhausting for those responsible for feeding the algorithms' insatiable appetite for new and interesting ideas. You can set your content marketing team up for success by not putting the lid on how many marketing messages you clarify and articulate in your messaging framework just because you only need a handful of benefit statements for a landing page, pop-up banner, or brochure right now.

Building a robust message library ensures your content creation teams will never be at a loss for what to say to your key audiences. Rather than spending valuable time trying to chase down busy executives and subject-matter experts throughout your company to interview and generate fresh topics, your content teams can effectively and efficiently help themselves to the reservoir of meaningful, preapproved content ideas and messages you've already created. In turn, they can more readily focus on turning those ideas into compelling content pieces and campaigns.

MESSAGE MAPS

A message map is a one-slide summary of one of your audiences and the offerings you provide them to satisfy their needs. Message maps briefly summarize the names and descriptions of an ICP (if you're a B2B brand) and a customer persona, including who they are, what they want, and what's in their way, along with the corresponding primary and supporting benefits for that customer segment, including features and advantages enabling those benefits. Like the five brand pillars that support your company or brand messaging and set your brand narrative apart from the competition, supporting benefits uphold your audience messaging. Think of them as audience pillars—secondary benefits that, when combined with the supporting features and advantages, form the short, explanatory paragraphs that follow your benefit headlines. We affectionately refer to these as "blurbs."

MESSAGE MAP	
ICP name (B2B brands)	
ICP description (B2B brands)	
Customer persona name	
Who they are	
What they want	
What's in their way	
Main benefit	
Supporting benefit *Features & advantages*	
Supporting benefit *Features & advantages*	
Supporting benefit *Features & advantages*	
Supporting benefit *Features & advantages*	

Benefit statements function as headlines in marketing copy, and each headline should have a supporting paragraph or blurb to go with it. You build blurbs by blending supporting benefit statements, or bullet points, together, along with their corresponding features and advantages. Pairing a benefit and a blurb creates *messaging blocks* you can stack on top of one another to form a *messaging stack*. You can use messaging stacks to build all kinds of marketing communications, including a web page, landing page, presentation, blog post, contributed article, or marketing collateral.

MESSAGING STACK		
Messaging block	Benefit	
	Blurb	
Messaging block	Benefit	
	Blurb	
Messaging block	Benefit	
	Blurb	
Messaging block	Benefit	
	Blurb	

The Messaging Funnel

Once you've organized your messaging framework, articulated your benefit statements, built your message maps, written your bullets and blurbs, and formed your messaging blocks and stacks, you're ready to develop your Messaging Funnel. The Messaging Funnel provides messages for all three stages of the marketing funnel, including the top of funnel (TOFU) stage, the middle of funnel (MOFU) stage, and the bottom of funnel (BOFU) stage.

Brand messaging addresses overarching problems and value propositions at the top of the funnel in the TOFU stage, where the focus is on addressing all your customers' overarching pain points without sales tie-ins. Audience-specific messaging and offering-specific messaging address audience-specific problems and overarching offerings for them in the MOFU stage, where you continue educating your customers on the criteria for a solution to their problems—criteria that point to your solution. Audience- and offering-specific messaging, the most granular and detailed type, corresponds to the bottom of your Messaging Funnel in the BOFU stage, where the goal is to engage one-on-one with sales-qualified leads who are actively seeking a specific solution to their problem, ideally using your solution criteria as previously outlined. Each level of messaging engages and progresses customers through their journey of learning about your solution to their problems.

The Backstory Messaging Funnel

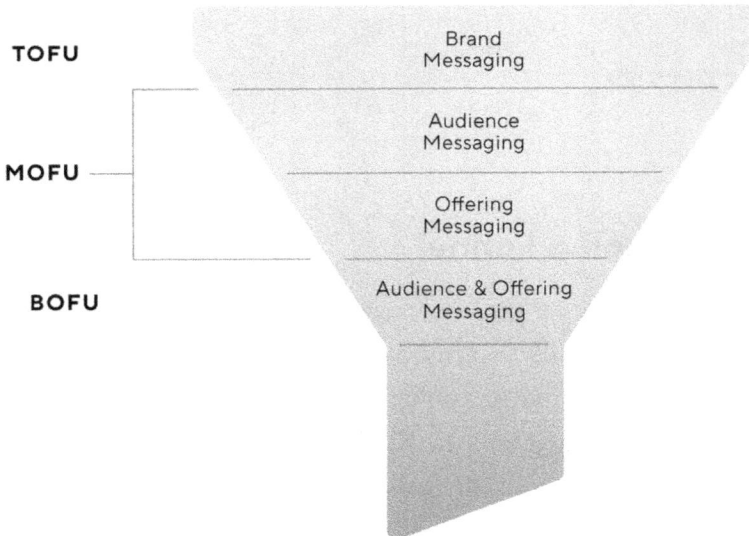

TOFU — Brand Messaging

MOFU — Audience Messaging / Offering Messaging

BOFU — Audience & Offering Messaging

The brand pillars you defined and articulated in Phase 2, Brand Foundation, are essential to creating and implementing content for your Messaging Funnel. Your brand pillars represent all five criteria required for solving your customers' problems and—by design—only your solution should be able to satisfy all of them. Generic table stakes category messaging will get you in the game, but it won't help you win. By defining the requirements for success, you give customers a shopping list that ultimately points them toward your solution. The Messaging Funnel guides customers through this process of discovery and realization, starting at the top of the funnel by educating them about a problem they have that costs them too much to ignore, followed by framing the five criteria for solving the problem that only your solution satisfies in the middle of the funnel. You've got to make it apparent to your customers that the pain they're experiencing from maintaining the status quo is far greater than the pain of change. The way you make this case should persuade and motivate customers to actively engage with your content, which will ultimately lead them to realize that only your solution satisfies all five criteria for success in solving their problem.

A strategic series of well-crafted, brand narrative–driven marketing messages can move marketing-qualified leads (MQLs) that match your Ideal Customer Profiles (ICPs) and personas toward becoming sales-accepted leads (SALs). SALs are those your sales team deems worth pursuing because they show clear buying signals and real potential. Generating more SALs doesn't just improve marketing ROI; it also accelerates sales velocity, boosts revenue growth, and drives profitability.

Effective marketing messaging does more than check boxes; it generates and converts customer demand for your solutions and services. The result is greater sales momentum and sustainable growth. It's the best of both brand and performance marketing—building awareness and preference for your brand while driving and qualifying customers through your marketing and sales pipeline. Just as importantly, it aligns your entire organization around a shared message, enabling teams to consistently create and deliver on the right customer expectations. That clarity leads to higher satisfaction, stronger loyalty, and longer-lasting customer relationships.

CHAPTER 11

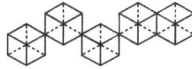

BRAND NARRATIVE

"We would be nothing without our story."

—Richard Branson

Watch what happens the next time you're at a networking event and people are introducing themselves to one another. It's surprising to see how rarely someone can answer this straightforward question: "What do you do?" Responses range from the misguided and meaningless to the overly detailed and drawn out. Striking the balance with a well-defined, intriguing response that elicits more interest and engagement is a rarity.

Think back to a time when you were preparing a proposal, writing an offer letter, creating an about us page for your website, or submitting your company for an award. How long did it take you to write a compelling description of your business and brand? How many back-and-forth discussions and revisions did it take to finalize? How different would that description have been if someone else from your organization had written it? How different will it be the next time you or someone else from your company writes it?

A compelling, intriguing, and consistent explanation of who you are, what you do, why it matters—and to whom—*is crucial to building a brand that scales*. Being ready to answer these foundational questions, both in spoken and written communication, goes a long way to setting you and your organization apart in meaningful, memorable ways. A strategic brand narrative consists of three parts: a one-line elevator pitch, a one-paragraph about us statement, and a one-page company overview. It takes about three seconds to share your elevator pitch, thirty seconds to read your about us statement, and three minutes to read your company overview. These three degrees of detail give you flexibility in meeting the demands of different situations and scenarios. Having each of them ready to go can facilitate meaningful connections with employees, customers, investors, and partners.

We'll break down each part of your brand narrative into its essential elements so you can build a compelling story and share the appropriate version of it when an opportunity presents itself—or when you proactively create one. The beauty of writing your brand narrative purposefully and proactively is that it's a compilation of everything you've defined up to this point. Yes, you will need to do some additional writing, but you can pull many of the inputs you'll need from material you've put together already.

Your Elevator Pitch

You don't have to be a Silicon Valley startup to benefit from having a compelling elevator pitch. Everyone ought to be able to briefly summarize what they do in twenty-five words or less in a way that elicits further interest, introductions, or referrals when the other person has a reason to care or knows someone who does.

Imagine getting on an elevator at an in-person conference. You don't know it yet, but an ideal customer for your company just got on the elevator with you. They see you're wearing a presenter's lanyard and say, "I'm trying to choose a breakout session. What's your talk about?" You're both getting off at the next floor, so you've only got a few seconds to make a great first impression, one that's compelling enough to make them want to come to your presentation. Would you be ready? Moments like these present themselves to us more often than we think. We never know when the person asking a question or listening in may be someone who can open an important door or make a valuable connection for us. A little preparation can go a long way in making the most of impromptu opportunities.

While working on-site at a client's office, I bumped into a high school friend I hadn't seen in years. He was a fellow runner. As it turns out, his office was across the hallway from my client. He explained he owned the commercial real estate development and management company that had built and still managed the Class-A office building and business park where my client's office was. When he asked what I was up to, I shared my elevator pitch with him, and he was interested in learning more, so he invited me to stop by his office that afternoon to discuss a project he was working on that related to what I do. That opportunistic conversation and connection resulted in four client engagements—including my friend's business—and additional referrals—worth a substantial sum of money, expanding my practice into a new industry, not to mention the reputational cachet.

Your elevator pitch should flow freely from the preparatory work you've done in the Brand Discovery and Brand Foundation phases because it blends elements of your brand purpose, position, and promise. Disruptive Advertising's Brand Foundation reads as follows, including the brand pillars we discussed in chapter 8:

- **Brand purpose:** To empower people and brands to remember and live in alignment with who they are.

- **Brand position:** The best performance marketing agency for authentic brands.

- **Brand promise:** Results in 90 days guaranteed.

- **Brand pillars:**

  ○ *Authenticity:* We only work with people and brands we believe in.

  ○ *Top Talent:* We hire, develop, and retain top talent you can trust.

  ○ *Strategy:* We align the right business goals to the right marketing strategy.

  ○ *Breakthroughs:* We leverage people, tools, and technology to deliver breakthrough results.

  ○ *Exclusivity:* We provide access to exclusive relationships, content, and community.

- **Brand personality:**

  ○ *Character:* Sage, Hero, Caregiver

  ○ *Visual:* Simple, bold, intuitive

  ○ *Voice:* Direct, inspiring, encouraging

And here is Disruptive Advertising's elevator pitch: "We're the best performance marketing agency for authentic brands and marketers." Everyone in their business knows and uses this elevator pitch when introducing the agency. These words resonate with prospective employees, customers, and partners, unlocking hearts and minds to new opportunities.

Your About Us Statement

Having defined your elevator pitch, you're ready to write your one-paragraph about us statement. Unlike a conversational elevator pitch meant to be spoken and heard, about us statements are designed to be written and read. They appear on the About tab of your company website, as boilerplate at the bottom of a press release, and as part of proposals, employment offers, and award submissions.

Writing your about us statement starts with creating a written version of your twenty-five-word elevator pitch. You should craft four versions of your about us statement, including a twenty-five-word version, a fifty-word version, a seventy-five-word version, and a hundred-word version. In doing so, you're prepared to introduce your business to different audiences in changing contexts on demand.

Disruptive Advertising's about us statement reads: "Disruptive Advertising is the best performance marketing agency for authentic brands and marketers. We align your business goals with the right marketing strategy and provide the people, tools, and technology to deliver breakthrough results. In addition, we give you access to exclusive relationships, content, and community. With over ten years of award-winning success and hundreds of five-star reviews, we guarantee a strategy that gives you confidence and impactful results without a long-term contract. If we don't deliver, you don't pay. At Disruptive, you win with a team you want to work with."

We've found it helpful to limit the number of words for an about us statement to no more than a hundred. This word-count constraint causes leaders to be thoughtful about what they say and rigorous in how they say it, the goal being to communicate a lot of meaning in just a few words. With the about us statement in place, you can add the other paragraphs needed to create your company overview.

Your Company Overview

Your one-page company overview builds on the about us statement and completes your brand narrative. Your five brand pillars provide additional insight and information for your overview. As a case in point, I've included in this section, with their permission, Disruptive Advertising's company overview. Each supporting paragraph begins with a power statement (italicized for easy reference) and has a complementary bookend that echoes that thought. Each paragraph is written to stand alone and works in concert with the other sections.

Inserted between your about us statement and brand pillar paragraphs is a paragraph that explains and educates the market about the problem you solve and its significance. As we discussed earlier, strategic brand narratives highlight a problem too big and costly to ignore and define five criteria for solving the problem that only your brand can fully satisfy in the form of your company overview. Disruptive Advertising's company overview addresses the issue of inauthentic brands and marketing, unpacking their costs and solving for them in its content marketing and Disruptive University personal and professional development training program.

Your company overview is a form of brand messaging that speaks to the value you deliver to customers at a high level. It helps get your audiences to lean in and want to learn more about the problems you solve for them, specifically through audience-specific messaging on your website and elsewhere. Remember, brand messaging is introductory and overarching company messaging. It's the kind of messaging you find on the home page of a website and at the top of your marketing funnel. Your company overview, or one-pager, frames your value in the context of who you serve, the main problems you solve for them, and a high-level overview of how you solve them. Having a one-pager that succinctly summarizes who you are, what you do, and why it matters is a big help to everyone who communicates on behalf of your business. It provides clear direction on what is and isn't on message for your organization and provides parameters for the core of your story.

About Disruptive Advertising

Disruptive Advertising is the best performance marketing agency for authentic brands and marketers. We align your business goals with the right marketing strategy and provide the people, tools, and technology to deliver breakthrough results. In addition, we give you access to exclusive relationships, content, and community. With over ten years of award-winning success and hundreds of five-star reviews, we guarantee a strategy that gives you confidence and impactful results without a long-term contract. If we don't deliver, you don't pay. At Disruptive, you win with a team you want to work with.

Authenticity: We only work with people and brands we believe in.

Because we only work with people and brands we believe in, you get the hearts and minds of our marketers—the discretionary part money can't buy—to achieve breakthrough results for your business. Authentic companies have a win-win-win mindset; they deliver great value for customers, develop their employees, and build healthy, sustainable businesses. Authentic marketers remember and live in alignment with who they are and support the brands they believe in. Pairing authentic brands and marketers is when the magic happens, and we test the limits of what's possible together.

Top Talent: We hire, develop, and retain top talent you can trust.

Building a winning marketing team is a full-time job that most businesses don't have the time or expertise to do. At Disruptive, we are experts at attracting, developing, and retaining authentic marketers. Our Disruptive University training and development program consistently results in breakthroughs in their personal and professional lives and amplifies their community impact. Connecting our top talent with people and brands they believe in is how we win together.

Strategy: We align the right business goals to the right marketing strategy.

For a strategy to be effective, you need a win-win-win goal, a realistic understanding of your current state, and a plan to bridge that gap. Through our Disruptive Difference process, we clarify your business goals and align them to an effective marketing strategy that drives immediate impact and sets us up for long-term success with data-informed decisions to improve the customer journey and optimize each marketing channel for better business results.

Breakthroughs: We leverage people, tools, and technology to deliver breakthrough results.

Without the right business goals, marketing strategy, and data, you can optimize any marketing channel and still lose. The Disruptive Difference connects the right people, tools, and technology with the information needed to drive breakthrough results. Beyond best practices and playbooks, our experts are constantly innovating and finding new ways to win.

Exclusivity: We provide access to exclusive relationships, content, and community.

Unlocking access to the right resources and relationships accelerates your personal growth, business success, and community impact. With Disruptive, you'll build lifelong relationships with your account team, attend invitation-only events with industry leaders, and collaborate with other authentic brands and marketers. Additionally, you'll gain access to our exclusive partner benefits and transformational content through Disruptive University and amplify the impact you have in your community through Disruptive Caring. By connecting authentic brands and marketers, we elevate the way business is done.

A well-crafted company overview makes writing copy for almost any communication piece or campaign easy because you have already defined what to say in narrative form. The copy for these downstream communication pieces and touch points practically writes itself because you've already done the heavy lifting. Like an aquifer that seeps water out of the side of a mountain, what starts as a trickle of ideas quickly converges into themes that form creeks and rivers of relevant information that sets you apart, differentiating your point of view in the competitive marketplace.

Taglines

Whether or not you need a tagline is up for debate. Taglines are optional in building your brand, but we prefer to include them when they help clarify what an organization stands for or does. In particular, brands with abstract names benefit from a concrete tagline that clearly and succinctly sums up their brand position or promise in just a few words.

Taglines are the most concise version of your brand story, a highly condensed reduction distilled from dozens of inputs, observations, and insights to just four to six words typically. Shaping a compelling brand story is like tying a bow tie with all the myriad inputs poured into one end and converging to a fine point in the middle, embodied in your tagline.

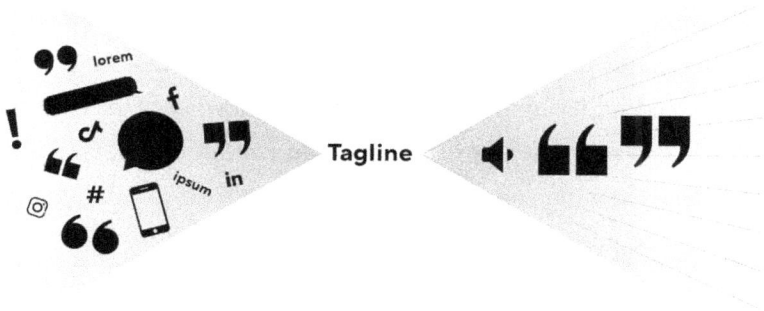

Like bouillon, your tagline is a highly concentrated form of your brand story. On one side of your tagline, the focus is on amplifying and leveraging the clear, concise messages you carefully crafted on the other side of your tagline, embodied in your messaging framework, message maps, and brand narrative, including your one-line elevator pitch, one-paragraph about us statement, and one-page company overview.

Some taglines make a simple yet profound value statement, which is not easy to articulate. Like Leonardo da Vinci said, "Simplicity is the ultimate sophistication." Disruptive Advertising's tagline, "Authenticity Wins," clearly and succinctly summarizes its positioning and brand promise in just two words. It helps underscore the agency's commitment to helping marketers live authentically by working with people and brands they believe in. It also challenges brands to do right by their employees, customers, and communities in an era when transparency reigns as a core value many customers and consumers hold in high esteem.

As another case in point, an off-handed comment from a thoughtful customer in an in-depth interview unlocked Claravine's tagline in just three words: "No Data Drama." He said, "I'm no copywriter, but

to me, they take the drama out of the data." Claravine's about us statement further expounds on this illuminating concept: "Claravine is The
Data Standards Company aiming to give people, teams, and technology a shared understanding of their data. Claravine helps brands and
agencies deliver on the promise of modern marketing by standardizing
taxonomies, naming conventions, and metadata across all digital experiences at the source of data creation."

Other taglines serve as a call to action that functions as a brand
mantra meant to inspire belief and attract and engage like-minded
audiences in a common cause. We recommended "Authenticity Wins"
as Disruptive Advertising's tagline to affirm their belief in the power
and necessity for marketers to be true to who they are by working for
people and brands they believe in and for companies to meet the needs
of their employees and customers in how they conduct business, not
just make more money. Brand mantras can be external or internal
facing, depending on the needs of the organization and the desired
outcomes they want to affect.

For DevPipeline, a company that facilitates insourced software
development for growing companies through competency-based
apprenticeships, the tagline we came up with was "Develop Your
Software Talent." This mantra-like tagline connects with and communicates the value DevPipeline provides to myriad audiences—including
apprentices, business owners and employers, civic leaders, and govern-
ment agencies. It also advocates DevPipeline's belief in the value of
apprenticeships as the only way to close the software talent gap (a big,
costly, undeniable problem) in which college degrees take too much
time and cost too much and bootcamps provide too little training and
hands-on experience, resulting in a million tech jobs going unfilled
each year.

The Copy Cascade

You'll be ready to write copy for your website after completing your elevator pitch, about us statement, and company overview. With these and the previously defined Brand Foundation elements in hand, including your messaging framework, message maps, and brand narrative, the copy for your website and other marketing communications practically writes itself.

Messaging is what to say, and copy is how to say it. Skilled copywriters will love inheriting your message maps, messaging stacks, and company overview. They'll know how to immediately translate them into copy, infusing the words with your brand voice as defined by your brand personality. The groundwork you've laid pays big dividends by accelerating the copywriting process for your website and other marketing communication pieces, including landing pages, ads, social media posts, presentations, collateral, content marketing, trade show graphics, webinars, and more.

Copywriters can use all the foundational messages you've articulated and clarified to create headlines and blurbs that quickly fill out and complete entire web pages. You'll probably still need to make some adjustments based on word choice preferences as you figure out how to apply your brand voice, but you will have already taken care of the heavy lifting. The momentum that flows from the clarity and confidence you have in your messaging will speed your time to market, avoiding lengthy debates about what to say. Making minor adjustments takes little time. Once you calibrate your brand voice, the words will flow with little need for time-consuming and smothering oversight.

It's not just copywriters who benefit from the work you've done to define your marketing messages. Everyone who communicates on behalf of your business in a market-facing role can leverage your messaging framework and company overview to create and deliver marketing messages to your audiences that are consistently on brand. The alignment that results from having a shared set of messages across your product, marketing, sales, and client success teams helps customers know what to expect from your offerings. When customers experience the promised benefits of a solution, they're more likely to keep using it. Customer loyalty is worth its weight in gold because you're leveraging your investment in acquiring those relationships and maximizing their lifetime value and recurring revenue. From this standpoint, the ROI on marketing messaging is one of your organization's most highly leveraged marketing activities because it touches many aspects of your business and makes a significant financial impact.

Building your brand narrative is essential to building a brand that scales. It's the culmination and convergence of all the elements you've defined up to this point in the brand-building process. Your brand narrative equips your team with what to say for every audience so they are never at a loss for words. They can now clearly and consistently communicate who you are, what you do, and why it matters. Putting your brand in words sets the stage for developing the additional elements of your Brand Expression, including your brand architecture, naming, visual brand identity, and the experiential aspects of your brand.

CHAPTER 12

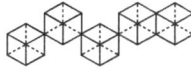

BRAND NAME AND
VISUAL BRAND IDENTITY

"Words have meaning, type has spirit."

—Paula Scher

Learning what makes brand names and visuals meaningful is a blessing and a curse. Once you become aware, you see missed opportunities everywhere: driving down the street, shopping at the grocery store, reading a restaurant menu, and watching the title sequence of a film. Of course, you see great examples, too, which inform good decisions when it's your turn to give clear, creative direction and make creative choices that serve your brand well.

What Is in a Name?

When asked why they gave their newborn son or daughter a certain name, I've heard parents say their child *looks* like that name. Other parents seem less constrained by matching a specific name to the look and feel of an individual than by creating a consistent family theme with their children's names: Janice, Jeffrey, Josie, and Jeremy.

Naming a brand that can scale and creating an appropriate visual brand identity for it should be a strategic, intentional process with the goal of reflecting the character and personality of the brand in a way that resonates with your customers. It should always be a name and identity the brand can grow into over time. It's all the more reason to thoughtfully answer the question "What does your brand want to be when it grows up?" before you've boxed it into a corner. Once you've established a brand name and imprinted its identity on your customers' minds, impressions and opinions can be difficult, if not impossible, to rewire.

To my mind, Jiffy Lube stands for oil changes, as its name suggests. Bolting "Multicare" onto the name as a brand extension hasn't changed my opinion of what the business does, even though I know the company wants me to think of them as doing more than just oil changes. As I mentioned earlier, it's like the guy who started as a plumber and then decided to expand his services by painting the words "electrical, HVAC, and more!" on his truck. It would have been better for these businesses to have anticipated the full suite of services they would offer at maturity before choosing a name too narrow to accommodate everything they eventually provided.

Naming Your Brand

As we discussed previously, brand names are capitalized proper nouns that we want to take the place of lowercase common nouns. They are the ideas and words we want our brands to become synonymous with in our customers' minds. The more your brand name suggests what you do, the faster those positive associations can connect your brand to your desired associations.

There are four main types of brand names: descriptive, suggestive, arbitrary, and fanciful. Descriptive names depict what a company is or does. For example, *Architectural Digest* is a monthly magazine focusing on landscaping and interior design. Suggestive names imply what a company is or does. For instance, Qualtrics is an experience management company that helps brands deliver better customer experiences by providing them with qualitative and quantitative customer research and analysis tools. Arbitrary names use real words in an unexpected context. Adobe, the software company, is a good example. Fanciful names are made-up words like Kodak or Xerox.

Additional naming classifications to be familiar with include names from different languages (think Prego spaghetti sauce) along with acronyms (a word formed from the initial letter or letters of a series of words in a phrase, as in GEICO and IKEA) and initialisms (a group of initial letters used as an abbreviation that does not form a word: BMW, CVS, and HSBC). Other naming conventions include truncated real words (Cisco, FedEx, MetLife), coined words (Coca-Cola, Google, Pentium), compound words (Allstate, DreamWorks, Facebook), and alphanumerics (3M, 7-Eleven, Porsche 911).[1]

Coming up with an ownable, effective brand name is paradoxical. The more unique a name is, the easier it is to register with the trademark office but the more time and resources it takes for it to stand for something meaningful in customers' minds. The more familiar a name is, the quicker customers understand it and the less likely it is to be distinctive enough to secure a trademark registration. Purely descriptive names can be too forgettable for customers to care about and remember and too common to be acceptable for examiners at the United States Patent and Trademark Office (USPTO), who are responsible for preventing brand names and visual brand identities from being mistaken for one another. Generally speaking, suggestive names can give you the ownability you need to register a trademark, if it's available in your classes of business, and a way to create faster connections to what you do in the minds of customers. Whatever type of name you choose, it's one thing to make a name; it's another thing entirely to make it matter.

THINK AUDIBLY FIRST WHEN IT COMES TO NAMING

Another important consideration in naming your brand is giving equal, if not greater, emphasis to how it sounds when spoken, not just how it looks in writing. We sometimes make the mistake of looking at name options only in written form when, in everyday life, we say and hear brand names more often than we see them. For this reason, it's important to listen to how a name sounds. Is it easy to understand, spell, repeat, and remember in the written form only? If not, you may want to keep looking for the right name.

As a guiding principle, giving your brand name a budget of no more than four syllables is a good idea. Syllables are expensive in terms of what they can cost you in connecting (or not) with your audience. Too many syllables in a name can cause people to abbreviate it, and for every fortunate abbreviation (FedEx), there are dozens of others that aren't. If people abbreviate your name and clump it into an indiscriminate alphabet soup of initialisms that function like a meaningless monogram, it can be easily mistaken and interchanged for another.

THINK TWICE BEFORE USING YOUR NAME

Think carefully about naming your business after yourself. When your business carries your name, it can create expectations in the minds of customers that you are the one they should talk to and prefer working with to get the full value of your services. Building a business that can operate without you is difficult if customers think they're getting second best when they're not dealing directly with you, the owner. Additionally, if you eventually want to sell your business, your name will go with it and selling your namesake is a high price to pay for any short-term gains from immediate name recognition out the gate.

Using a different name gives you the option of selling the business without any perceived loss in value from customers. Like when Westley takes over the business and role of the Dread Pirate Roberts in *The Princess Bride*, you can pass your business on to the next person to run or even own it, independent of your direct involvement, without losing any cachet.

BRAND ARCHITECTURE

Defining a brand architecture provides naming guidelines for your company and its offerings. Two strategies bookend the naming continuum: a branded house and a house of brands with varying shades of endorsement in between. A branded house strategy applies the same name to all your offerings to create shared associations among them—think Kirkland Signature, Costco's private-label store brand that does more annual revenue than Nike.[2] The goal of a branded house strategy is to transfer the positive perceptions customers have with one product to its sibling products. In the case of Kirkland Signature, those positive associations extend across far-ranging categories from bath tissue to cashews to trash can liners.

A house of brands naming strategy, on the other hand, gives each product a unique name that sets it apart, devoid of any apparent family relationship. The purpose is to attract different kinds of customers who identify with different brand values—think Luxottica's portfolio of over 150 eye care products (Barberini, Crizal, Essilor, and Transitions), eyewear (Chanel, Oakley, Ray-Ban, and Swarovski), and direct-to-consumer brands (LensCrafters, Target Optical, and Pearle Vision in North America, along with others in other markets).

Between these two naming strategy bookends are degrees of endorsement that range from subtle shadow endorsements—where brands go by different names even though consumers know they're owned by the same parent company—to overt parent brand naming relationships. In these cases, every brand in the portfolio carries the same parent brand name as a reference point for all the brands attached to it.

The question at the heart of brand architecture and naming strategy is how closely associated you want your brands to be with one another. The stronger you want the associations to be, the more similar the names of your company and offerings will be to one another. Suppose a new brand has the potential to tarnish the stellar reputation of an established brand. In that case, adopting a house of brands approach allows you to tear away the new brand along the perforation between the different types of names, should it fail, without damaging the established brand with unwanted contagion. Taking a hybrid approach is another option for building out your brand architecture. In cases where you've got multiple product lines with shared ingredients, attributes, or purposes, consider creating a different naming theme for each product line. Having multiple product lines with different naming themes combines elements of a branded house and a house of brands.

That's a lot to remember, and perhaps you'll choose a subset of these guidelines to inform your naming process. Even if you don't try to follow all of them, having some objective parameters that provide bumper pads to keep the decision-making process headed in the right direction is better than letting the process devolve into a patchwork of episodic names that have no rhyme or reason. Remember this guiding principle: view your brand name from your customers' perspectives. Is the name going to resonate with them and help them develop the perception you want them to have of your brand? If your boss, brother, or spouse isn't the customer, it doesn't matter whether they like the name.

Visual Brand Identities

Designing a visual brand identity that can scale with your business as it grows starts by defining a clear brand strategy, including its brand personality. Without a clear strategic direction for your brand, selecting a logo design can default to personal preference and decision by committee—the worst method of all. Instead, use objective criteria to guide the design evaluation process to create a logo that reflects your desired brand perception. You can tell whether the design process is strategic or not by listening to the way decision-makers respond to proposed designs. Personalized comments such as "I don't like it" indicate a lack of strategic direction, whereas feedback that takes the design criteria into account reflects a strategic approach.

Other design aspects to consider include the legibility of the logo from a distance, in color and black and white, against different background colors, at a reduced size, and applied to various materials and media for signage, embroidered apparel, swag, and digital applications, including your website, software applications (if applicable), and email signatures. Logos that look great in one context may fail to communicate in another.

Early versions of your logo that were appropriate for your initial audience and stage of growth may not resonate with new audiences as your business evolves. In the process of rebranding DemoChimp to Consensus, the leading B2B demo automation platform, I helped the company go from the DemoChimp logo, which featured a playful-looking monkey designed with SMBs (small- and medium-sized companies) in mind to a sophisticated-looking *C* icon made from a series of intersecting lines that suggested the convergence and agreement Consensus facilitates. The new logo supported the new Consensus brand position as a solution for savvy customers at large companies like Oracle and SAP.

Had the company anticipated it would grow to serve enterprise customers, it could have created a name and logo appropriate for that audience from the beginning. It took a few pivots for the business to find its ideal customer. When it did, the brand also needed to pivot to connect with and convert the right buyers. Interestingly, the Consensus name and logo don't dissuade SMBs from using the platform, so the company was able to go up market without losing its original base. Garin Hess, the founder and CEO of the company, said the Consensus brand name doubled the value of the business because it framed the problem the company solves and the value it provides in a much more intuitive way, making it easier for customers, analysts, and investors to buy into his vision to create the demo automation category, which Consensus leads today.

demochimp™

 **consensus**

ONE PURPOSE, TWO TYPES OF VISUAL BRAND IDENTITY

Referring to a logo as a visual brand identity is a reminder that a brand is more than a logo; it's the sum total of all the impressions a brand has made through the words, images, and experiences it has created for audiences, resulting in the perceptions they have. It would be amazing if your ideal customers loved your brand entirely, and that is the ultimate goal of branding, but when everyday people say they love your brand, what they're typically referring to is your logo.

Wordmarks and logomarks are the two major design classifications of logo designs. As their names suggest, wordmarks are logos based on typographic treatments of brand names, whereas logomarks include symbols or images in addition to the name of a company or offering. The Google logo is a wordmark. The Nike Swoosh is a logomark that has become so ubiquitous as to not need the word "Nike" next to it, much like single-name singers: Adele, Beyoncé, Bono, and Elvis. Granted, it takes a long time and a lot of relevant product and brand marketing to drop your brand name in favor of a symbol-only logo. Nike used a name-logo lockup for decades before using the Swoosh as a stand-alone element in its brand communication. Once its brand became ubiquitous, Nike began using the Nike name and Swoosh together to signify lifestyle-oriented products versus Swoosh-only performance products using the latest product technology and design innovations. When Nike introduces a more innovative product, it downgrades its predecessor products and moves them into the Nike Swoosh lifestyle realm.

Some logos, like Carhartt, combine a stylized type element with a distinctive icon or type treatment. Coca-Cola trademarked its logo in 1905. A bookkeeper named Frank Mason Robinson named the syrup for the soda by combining words inspired by two of its key ingredients:

"coca" from coca leaves and "cola" from kola nuts. The Coca-Cola Company became an official Georgia corporation in 1892. In addition to being the company's bookkeeper, Robinson also designed the company's world-famous logo, writing out the name Coca-Cola in Spencerian script, the style of penmanship popular among bookkeepers at the time.[3]

Factors that inform whether to choose a logomark or a wordmark include the diversity of audiences your brand serves. Building a brand that has or will have an international presence points to choosing an icon-driven logomark that needs no verbal explanation or interpretation. Other factors include the competitive landscape for your specific category and whether an icon will set you apart or make you blend in. If you want to stand out, doing something different when it comes to visually communicating your brand can help, but it still needs to be relevant. Your logo should convey your brand personality and resonate with the audiences you serve.

DON'T BE AFRAID TO CALL YOUR BABY UGLY

Be sure to get critical feedback on your logo design from people who understand your market, have good taste, and aren't afraid to call your baby ugly. The first version of the Grow logo wasn't working. It was supposed to look like a seedling, but instead, it looked like a matchstick. To his credit, Grow's founder and former CEO, Rob Nelson, asked the designer to try again. The resulting logo is much more unique, interesting, emotive, and engaging. Its circular design and undulating waves are reminiscent of the dynamic growth curves of the companies using Grow's business intelligence platform to democratize data-driven decision-making. In other words, it's on brand.

GROW

GROW

When Human Services HQ rebranded to BambooHR in 2013, the product-first company worked with a top-tier design firm to create an elegant logo and website design, even though the business was still young. Ryan Sanders, cofounder and head of product and operations, advocated for investing in good design early on, and his cofounder and partner, Ben Peterson—who led sales and marketing—backed him all the way. Ryan said the company rebranded because "after a year, it became evident that no one could remember our company name—including our clients, potential customers, and even my wife. This posed a significant problem."

Ben and Ryan believed they were building a great brand and business and invested in a great name and design accordingly. "BambooHR" brought positive connotations to the brand name even though it didn't directly speak to what the company does—other than the direct HR reference. Sanders explains, "Bamboo has been used worldwide for centuries. It embodied qualities such as being green, flexible, and renewable. Upon adopting the Bamboo name, the response was immediate. Everyone remembered it."[4]

Furthermore, Ben and Ryan decided to concentrate exclusively on creating human resources software for small- and medium-sized businesses. They understood the value of looking like the category leader they wanted to become. It was a self-fulfilling prophecy as the company went from having thirty employees at its rebrand to over one thousand employees today with more than $100 million in annual recurring revenue.

OWN A COLOR

Considering the associations color theory assigns to the color palette,[5] it's not surprising certain industries gravitate toward some colors and not others. For example, businesses in the financial services industry often choose blue as their signature brand color.

- Red: powerful, passionate, loving

- Yellow: hopeful, cheerful, optimistic

- Orange: flamboyant, warm, stimulating

- Green: renewing, refreshing, regenerating

- Blue: trustworthy, dependable, committed

- Purple: mystic, royal, creative

- Black: sophisticated, dramatic, elegant

- White: clean, pure, innocent

- Gray: refined, dignified, conservative

- Brown: stable, solid, approachable

- Pink: romance, sweetness, happiness

In our work for the accounting and advisory firm Tanner, our design partner, Bill Chiaravalle, specified orange as the company's new signature color to convey a sense of dynamic leadership and vitality. Paired with the firm's iconic owl mascot logo, orange set the firm apart from local and regional professional services firms. It even differentiates it on a national level where global providers had staked out ownership of other colors: EY commandeered yellow, Deloitte owned green, Accenture embraced purple, and KPMG claimed blue.

As Bill and I explain in Tanner's brand style guide, "The Tanner owl symbol is the primary visual representation of the visual brand. The owl was a Greek symbol of Athena, the goddess of wisdom and strategy. According to myth, an owl sat on Athena's blind side so that she could see the whole truth. The owl symbol represents the wisdom, good judgment, knowledge, keen insight, and intuition that embody the collective team of accountants and advisors at Tanner." As you can see from this example, it's important to consider your brand strategy in the context of your competitive landscape both now and into the future.

Cultural and competitive context are key considerations in picking your signature brand color. Depending on the kind of perception you're trying to create and what color will help reinforce it, consider the connotation color holds for your audience based on their cultural context, the experiences other industry players provide for them, and how those competitors are trying to shape customer perceptions. Choosing a color for your brand consistent with your desired perception while considering the larger market context can help you see potential unintended customer interpretations.

Visual, Verbal, and Experiential Brand Guidelines

Empowering your visual brand communications team with clear and consistent rules for the correct use of your brand logo, typography, color palette, patterns, and visual imagery is essential to creating effective visual brand communications. Brand style guides serve this purpose, along with brand tone of voice guidelines for written and verbal communication. You can find good examples of these documents online. The "Voice and Tone" section of the Mailchimp Content Style Guide is one of the most robust examples of a comprehensive set of brand tone of voice guidelines.[6] The breadth and depth of its coverage go beyond what many brands want or need, but it's a great example nonetheless.

Experiential brand guidelines are another key component of consistently setting up your brand for success across customer touch points in Phase 4, Brand Activation. Experiential guidelines cover far-ranging topics specific to each business, such as how the company should greet customers and vendors in person and over the phone, welcome on-site visitors, format and give presentations, dress to represent the business at the office and traveling for business, provide campus tours, host guest speakers, clean restrooms and other facilities, prepare and reset meeting rooms, take clients to dinner, package welcome boxes and swag items, and so on. Everything your employees do communicates something positive or negative about your brand in the creation of your designed brand perception, making it critical to think through the details of the experiences you create for your employees and customers.

Brand Culture

Culture Partners, the renowned culture of accountability consultancy, has a simple yet powerful framework for leveraging your investment in creating a compelling and effective company culture. The Results Pyramid shows the interdependency among experiences, beliefs, actions, and results to highlight the significance of inspiring and motivating your employees to live your brand values in everyday interactions with one another and your customers and partners. Cultural beliefs stem from the experiences employees have with them, which makes it all the more worthwhile to create culture-defining experiences that change your employees' beliefs and mindsets and put them on a path to take different and better actions for different and better results.

Aristotle famously said something to the effect of "We are what we repeatedly do." The best modern-day definition of culture I've found is from Culture Partners, and it echoes Aristotle's sentiment: "Culture is how we think and what we do. It's the beliefs, values, and behaviors of an organization." If you don't codify your culture by clearly articulating the beliefs and behaviors that define it, you're leaving a vacuum for others to fill, and you might not like where they take it.

In defining your company culture, don't default to cliché statements that don't truly align with what motivates or inspires you and your team. Let this be more than an obligatory checkbox exercise that satisfies some mandatory activity at an executive retreat. Instead, dig deep to discover and define the shared characteristics of the people who embody your company at its best and take the time to articulate the beliefs and behaviors that define the common denominators among them. Remember, your company ought to be demonstrating your values today in substantial ways—perhaps not as consistently as you'd like, but not so infrequently as to make them totally aspirational either.

We've found that the most effective way to codify an organization's culture is to share stories about the people who embody your culture at its best and reverse engineer how they think and what they do to get results. Values can be expressed as one-word nouns that define the beliefs and behaviors that have the biggest impact on helping your organization live up to your brand promise every day. Fifty examples of values include the following from James Clear, author of *Atomic Habits*, and his collaborative work with the LeaderShape Institute.[7]

EXAMPLES OF CORE VALUES				
Accountability	Calmness	Dependability	Honesty	Reputation
Achievement	Challenge	Determination	Humor	Respect
Adventure	Commitment	Entertainment	Innovation	Responsibility
Altruism	Community	Equality	Integrity	Security
Ambition	Compassion	Excellence	Love	Selflessness
Authenticity	Competency	Fairness	Loyalty	Service
Authority	Courage	Fellowship	Openness	Spirituality
Balance	Creativity	Forgiveness	Optimism	Stewardship
Beauty	Curiosity	Fun	Personal Development	Trustworthiness
Boldness	Decisiveness	Health	Pleasure	Wisdom

While not exhaustive, this list will hopefully spark some ideas for defining your own values. In our experience, values are most effective when they grow out of the lived experiences of the leaders and members of your organization. Stories from your own company culture illustrate your values and bring them to life. We don't recommend borrowing values from other companies, no matter how much success they've had with them. Your values should reflect *your* unique culture. If they're only aspirational and not a true reflection of your culture today, your employees may become cynical when you try to discuss them, which will only hurt your credibility and cost you their trust and confidence.

Having defined your core values, you'll want to write a short sentence for each that inspires your employees to put them into practice. Dropping the value noun and simply referring to the values in sentence form can make your values feel more action-oriented. Strong company cultures are self-correcting in that their employees notice when a team member's behaviors aren't consistent with their values. I'm not suggesting employees police one another, but when a staff member is clearly out of step with the values you've taught and trained people to live by, it can be helpful when employees encourage one another to get back in alignment.

No matter the size of your company, brand culture stories can be a powerful way to transmit your cultural values to new team members and partners. Initially, these stories may come from the founders or Hall of Fame employees. However, as you expand your brand culture circle to include more people and recognize and reward those who live your values, more team members will begin to build their own stories based on their experiences living your organization's shared beliefs and behaviors. Being intentional about capturing these stories, writing them down, and even creating videos about them will help cultivate the kind of company culture you want to have rather than hoping a poster on the wall in the break room will make a difference.

Initially, leaders within organizations seed the development and adoption of a culture with stories illustrating the application of their values and showing the benefits of putting the organization's beliefs and behaviors to work. While the initial seeding stage is important, the goal is for other executives, managers, and individual contributors to put your values into practice for themselves and create their own stories. When they start to develop and share their own brand culture stories, you'll know your values are becoming embedded in the hearts and minds of the people who work with you.

Building a Brand Book

A brand book encapsulates the elements of your Brand Foundation and culture in one place. It becomes a source of inspiration and direction in guiding your employees and partners on who you are and what you stand for to protect your brand and teach your team how to be effective brand ambassadors. Unlike a brand style guide outlining rules for using your visual brand identity correctly, a brand book summarizes your brand purpose, brand position, brand promise, brand pillars, and brand personality. In addition, it outlines and summarizes the values, beliefs, and behaviors that define your brand culture. Distributing a digital version of your brand book is often sufficient without the need to print it in physical form.

Trademark Registrations

Speaking of protectability, don't cut corners when registering your brand name and logo. To think you can get away with not registering your brand name or logo with the United States Patent and Trademark Office is shortsighted and risky. Just ask anyone who has received a cease-and-desist letter mandating they stop using a brand name in which they've invested valuable time and money.

A client of ours who forgot to register the name of their business received just such a letter and had to rebrand mid–hockey stick. Sales were skyrocketing, and the complexities of scaling the business were already taxing the company's leadership and infrastructure. Having to come up with a new name and visual identity in the middle of that hypergrowth was challenging, to say the least. They successfully transitioned to a great new name and visual brand identity without compromising their growth opportunities. Still, it would have been a lot easier to have researched the availability of their name and registered it in their classes of business from the beginning.

Keep in mind that the USPTO groups similar products and services together in business classes or categories that guide the trademark review and registration process. These categories are meant to reflect the way customers organize products and services in their minds to avoid confusion between your offerings and those of others. You must register your trademark in all the classes of business that pertain to your brand and the way you take it to market. The examiner assigned to your application at the USPTO will make the call as to whether or not your trademark is descriptive, meaning that it merely describes what something is or does, or unique, thus determining whether or not it could confuse customers.

In addition to registering your brand name and logo in the classes of business that apply to your brand in the United States, it's also important to consider registering your brand in the international markets where you'll be doing business. Don't let an opportunistic or bad actor scoop up your name and squat on it, extorting payment before relinquishing it to you or blocking your use of it in that market altogether.

After you've checked the clearance to market for your brand name in your classes of business, do a Google search to see how it's being used in the marketplace today. If a significant company already uses your name, consider finding another one, even if the company hasn't registered it. General practice states that if a company started using a name before your registration, that company can continue using it even after you've secured your trademark registration, though it won't be able to prevent you from using it. These are just suggestions based on our experience. Please consult with your trademark attorney to verify these guidelines for your situation.

Coordinating all your brand expressions is a big job. If you're the founder of a company still early in its development and you still wear the marketing hat, you'll need to lead by example, bringing your brand to market in a clear, consistent way. If you have a full-time head of marketing, they will take the lead in ensuring everyone understands your brand and represents it well in their respective areas of responsibility.

BRAND ACTIVATION

"Every interaction, in any form, is branding."

—Seth Godin

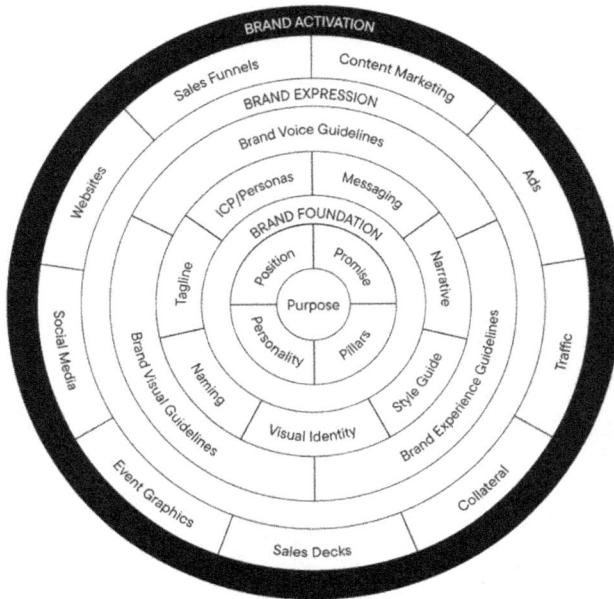

Walking through the Niketown store on Michigan Avenue in downtown Chicago in the mid-1990s felt like walking through an immersive brand book. The graphics, product displays, and people were highly aligned and attuned to the Nike brand ethos at a level few brands achieve or even conceive. I remember seeing a fractional graphic of Scottie Pippen become a complete picture as I rode up the escalator. It was an interactive art exhibit and optical illusion all in one. I also remember having a genuine conversation with a sales guy in the basketball shoe department, complete with a basketball hoop, mini wood basketball floor, and a painted key and free throw line where you could try out some sneakers while taking some shots and talking shop.

I asked the b-ball sales rep where I could catch a game of streetball, and after sizing me up, he had some immediate recommendations that were on point. Similarly, though in a very different category, working with Sportsman's Warehouse taught us the importance of having salespeople who live the brand behind the counter as well as in real life. These are people who actually use the products they're selling. Their firsthand experience allows them to be authentic, credible, and persuasive to technical customers who are looking for an opportunity to show what they know—and learn something new—in the process of buying guns, fishing poles, and gear. The same holds true for customer-facing salespeople of software and services. When your salespeople aren't knowledgeable or passionate about your brand and offerings, it shows. And, of course, the opposite is true.

As we've discussed, branding creates the words, images, and experiences that influence customers' perceptions of your brand. To influence your desired brand perception, you've got to consistently reinforce your brand through every interaction and take advantage of every opportunity to make a favorable impression on customers. Even after experiencing standout examples of brands doing things right, it can still be a struggle to replicate similar results when assuming responsibility for building a brand of your own. Still, you can learn a lot by observing and paying attention to brands that resonate.

Disney's theme parks are renowned for having all their cast members (employees) stay in character as they do their work. A retail worker in a souvenir shop at Disneyland in Anaheim told me she didn't smile much at home because her smile needed to recuperate from having to be used so much at work in keeping with the Disney brand.

Disneyland dresses its sidewalk sweepers in costumes that blend in with the park aesthetic, and they go about their work with a cheerful disposition and sense of urgency you'd expect to see at the happiest place on earth. Even Disneyland has its loopholes. Backstage tours of Disneyland reveal inconspicuous passageways where Disney characters can move quickly from one park area to another or take a break. Multiple people dress up as the same character during peak times at the park.

When my kids were young, we were in line to meet Minnie Mouse at Disneyland. We patiently waited our turn, and just as we got to the front of the line, a cast member stepped between my daughter and Minnie, saying, "I'm sorry, but Minnie is on break." We were disappointed but pushed on to see the next character who was nearby, Ariel from *The Little Mermaid.* As we approached her location, Miranda, who was five at the time, said, "That's okay, Dad. Ariel can't walk away; she has flippos!"

Other brick-and-mortar brands are stepping up and experimenting with different customer experience models. Customer-oriented grocery stores have more team members on the floor than budget stores. These employees will walk with you to the shelf and point out the item you're looking for. Personal shoppers text for permission to substitute an item for curbside pickup when it's out of stock. Airlines allow you to get a callback when wait times are "longer than expected." LiDAR (light detection and ranging) technology is helping Coca-Cola bottlers optimize the product mix based on dynamic data at the point of sale instead of simply slinging products on shelves to match static planograms.

Digital-first and digital-only brands are doing everything they can to develop their own customer databases by giving customers reasons to share more about themselves. By engaging with them directly through zero- and first-party data interactions, brands can enrich customer profiles, enhance customer engagement, and boost revenue. The stakes for controlling customer data have never been higher as brands seek to compete with Apple and the other members of the Big Five: Alphabet, Amazon, Meta, and Microsoft.

Managing the customer experience and their expectations across all your brand touch points requires a significant investment in tools, training, collaboration, and coordination. Learning where to invest and continually improving the experience is a never-ending process. Knowing who your most valuable customers are and investing at the appropriate levels for the relative value of each segment is half the battle. The other half is making sure your teams, both internal and external, understand who those customers are, what they're worth to your business, what they want, and how to position and communicate your brand to become the obvious choice for meeting their needs in an emotionally satisfying way.

When you provide your team with clearly defined brand standards and create a culture that commits to consistently following them throughout your Brand Activation activities, it's like having your team ride together in a peloton, drafting behind a shared understanding of your brand that breaks the wind and pulls them forward instead of having to ride into a headwind on their own. Without clarity, something as simple as writing a proposal can be a chore as you struggle to describe what your business does and how it's different. In fact, an executive at a client of ours, Epcon Partners, a professional staffing agency for energy-related infrastructure construction projects, commented on how quickly proposals come together when you already know what to say about your brand. With The Backstory Brand Wheel Framework leading the way, you always know what to say and how to say it.

As we discuss further in chapter 13, "Customer Touch Points," the ultimate aim of the Brand Activation phase of the brand-building process is to build your brand while building your business. Some would have you think these goals are at odds with each other, that it's an either-or proposition, but we disagree. We believe in blending both brand *and* performance marketing simultaneously so you get the best of both worlds. Yes, it takes more insight, strategy, planning, and coordination, but it's what the best brands do, and you can too.

CHAPTER 13

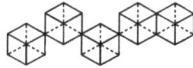

CUSTOMER TOUCH POINTS

*"Your brand is a story unfolding across
all customer touch points."*

—Jonah Sachs

Creating and maintaining alignment in bringing your brand to life is a never-ending process because circumstances and inputs constantly change. Painting crews continually work on the Golden Gate Bridge to protect it from the corrosive salty air of the San Francisco Bay. Consistently and effectively activating your brand requires constant focus, detailed attention, and continual refreshing.

Every interaction between you and your brand is a customer touch point. Like the individual splotches of color in an impressionistic painting, the personal impressions from all your brand touch points meld in customers' hearts and minds to form an overall picture of your brand and a feeling that gives customers confidence in buying and recommending your brand—or not.

Because everyone who works for your organization creates or contributes to customer touch points in some way, branding is everyone's responsibility, not just the marketing team's. Educating all your team members on what to say about your brand and how to represent it visually and experientially throughout all your touch points helps build a robust and protective brand reputation to get where you want to go.

Inconsistencies between your brand promise and the lived experience you deliver to customers can detract from the perception and reputation of your brand. These brand gaps matter most for customer segments worth more to your organization. Scoring the relative value of your customer relationships, as we explored in chapter 3, helps prioritize which relationships matter most and which gaps to focus on closing first. Investing proportionately against your most valuable customers starts by understanding that not all relationships are equally important. Of course, your most valuable audience is the employees who create and deliver your customer experience. Making sure they're well taken care of is your priority. Doing so will help them buy into your brand so they go beyond meeting the bare minimum requirements to willingly give the kind of discretionary creativity and effort that separates great brands from good ones.

BambooHR built a brand that scales by articulating and living values that attract like-minded employees and customers. Though counterintuitive for a SaaS startup, the company's founders made it clear they *didn't* want their employees working after hours or on weekends.

Instead, they wanted their team members to enjoy spending time with family and friends and come back to work refreshed and ready to go—and they wanted the same opportunity for themselves. They'd seen too many SaaS companies and founders burn out and suffer from bankrupt relationships at work and home, and they didn't want to repeat those life-altering lessons.

Brand performance marketing: The outermost ring of The Backstory Brand Wheel Framework, Brand Activation, focuses on creating and executing customer touch points to generate profitable growth and revenue for your business. You can meet your performance marketing objectives without sacrificing your brand-building efforts. All the elements in the Brand Activation phase should work together to simultaneously build your business and brand as an integrated whole. Building your brand from the center of the Brand Wheel to the next ring is the best way to ensure your Brand Activation activities are purposeful, aligned, and effective.

You first developed a foundational understanding of your brand by defining your brand purpose, brand position, brand promise, brand pillars, and brand personality. You followed with the work in the second section of the Brand Wheel, Brand Expression. As a result, your brand has a helm and rudder you can use to deliberately steer it toward your desired destination as you transition into Brand Activation activities instead of letting the current take you where it wants to go.

As the Brand Foundation heading suggests, the elements within the inner circle of your Brand Wheel change very little from year to year. Whereas the outermost Brand Activation elements can change quite often depending on the degree to which your company and competitors are innovating and developing new offerings and new ways of marketing them. Different elements of the Brand Expression section of your Brand Wheel may evolve at different speeds as your company grows, shifts its customer focus, expands its offerings, or responds to changing competitive pressures.

Brand Activation activities and deliverables are generally the most well-understood aspects of marketing. Each of these elements in your marketing plan and go-to-market strategy will be more effective and impactful when you have done the necessary Brand Discovery, Brand Foundation, and Brand Expression work to be clear and confident in what to communicate in activating your brand.

Leveraging your message library: Your investment of time, attention, and effort in defining your ICPs, messaging framework, message maps, and brand narrative in the Brand Expression phase of work is ongoing and pays big dividends throughout all aspects of Brand Activation. Since you've already defined who your audiences are, what to say to them, and how your brand should look, sound, and feel, your teams can adapt, fly in formation, and quickly get new team members, contractors, freelancers, and partners up to speed on what to say and how to say it. You can consistently create on-message and on-brand content for each of your audiences and offerings with confidence—at scale—without having to constantly check everyone's work for accuracy or alignment or be surprised by what your team releases into the wild.

When and why to use AI: We recommend using AI tools to blend your own differentiated messaging ingredients rather than relying on AI to generate full-formed copy from scratch. When content is crowd-sourced from the internet's shared idea pool, it leads to derivative thinking, average messaging, recycled knowledge, and copycat concepts. The result? Undifferentiated blather. Imagine being limited to the same set of words to draw from as your competitors—like having a finite set of refrigerator magnets you and everyone else in your industry simply rearrange in different configurations without saying anything truly different. Instead, you should create differentiated, proprietary content that conveys your uncommon knowledge and insights by diving deep to understand how customers perceive your brand and why, along with how to talk with them about your unique products and offerings in singular and engaging brand, audience, and offering messaging.

Once you've defined the features, advantages, and benefits of your offerings for each of your key audiences, you can save time by using AI tools to combine or reimagine these elements into pithy and differentiated paragraphs or blurbs to support your benefit headlines and set you apart. Using this method, and with a bit of editing, you can quickly create and repurpose chunks of content without compromising quality.

Be sure to choose a system that doesn't allow your hard-won insights to indiscriminately leak out into the collective pool of content. Use a tool that protects your insights from becoming common knowledge and keeps them contained in your own secure work environment. The last thing you want is to hand your playbook to a competitor, undermining the differentiated positioning and messaging you've worked so hard to clarify. Protecting those insights is key to fueling distinct, high-impact content across your marketing touch points.

Websites: Your website is the centerpiece of your performance brand marketing efforts. Designing and building a great-looking website with clear, concise, cohesive messages, and a great user experience will ensure your site can quickly communicate your value, convert the right customers, and engage them in wanting to learn more about your solution. Well-designed website pages are like appetizers for your product entrée. If your appetizers look or taste bad, figuratively speaking, customers might not stick around long enough to try the main course.

For your home page copy, you can draw ideas and content from your brand narrative. For your solutions pages, find inspiration from your message maps and identify the top five benefits for each audience and offering. When you're never at a loss for what to say, you can move quickly and confidently through the copywriting process for your website, using this three-step process:

1. Create a basic wireframe that maps out what goes where for each page of your site, including your calls to action (CTAs). It's here that you map out the user experience (UX).

2. Once you know what goes where, write the copy for each section of each page using benefit statements as headlines and an appropriate AI tool, if you like, to blend supporting benefits and their associated advantages and benefits to quickly create and edit explanatory paragraphs or blurbs. Of course, writing blurbs by hand ensures unique Brand Expression with the most opportunity to infuse your brand tone of voice into your content.

3. Design your site to get your ideas across in the most visually appealing and engaging way possible with a user interface (UI) design that follows the guidelines for your visual brand identity and style guide.

Digital marketing: The most effective digital marketing campaigns and programs are idea driven. They go beyond throwing ideas against the wall or A/B testing which ads and content convert best. They build momentum around a big idea that gives customers a reason to care and click, a strategic concept that is creative, engaging, and relevant across all the touch points of your customer journey. Analytics, measurement, and attribution are essential elements of measuring the effectiveness of your marketing strategy. You can't expect customers to pay attention to your marketing if it lacks an underlying insight into who they are, what they want, and what's in the way, along with clearly and articulately communicating your unique ability to address those issues.

Having laid the groundwork for insightful content and copywriting, you're prepared with a robust message library to produce quality content at scale and sustain a steady content creation rhythm. You can think of it like a fully stocked pantry that allows you to make and bake whatever you want as your menu of content needs evolves from one audience and channel combination to another. Expecting your team to scrape your website or other marketing collateral as if to gather messaging ingredients from which to make other marketing communication deliverables is like asking a chef to extract the salt, flour, and baking soda from a loaf of bread to make cookies. At best, it's inefficient, and at worst, it sets them up for failure. How are they supposed to know which messages are meant for certain audiences and which messages matter most to each of them?

SEO: It takes at least six months to start to see the fruits of your SEO labors, but building your online authority to generate good search results on an ongoing basis is a significant advantage and asset to your business. Doing basic keyword research is just the beginning. You've got to weave those keywords into relevant, conversational content through topics that reach and engage your audiences to make your brand relevant. Savvy marketers and business leaders don't cut corners when building real authority online. They create quality content to answer real customers' questions in genuine, relatable ways, giving authoritative sites a reason to link to yours and elevating your online presence. Here again, your message library is a reservoir of relevant ideas, messages, and information to draw from in creating content that continually refreshes your online presence. Creating link-worthy content you can infuse with keywords in natural ways gives the SEO algorithms a reason to rank your site higher in search results.

Display advertising: At the top of the funnel, you've got a great opportunity to educate customers about the problem you solve for them and why they can't afford to ignore it, along with the five criteria for success that only your brand and business can fully satisfy. Running display ads on the Google Display Network (GDN) intercepts customers as they navigate through sites that may not have anything to do with the problem you solve for them. They may not even know they have the problem or why they should care, which is even more reason to create compelling content based on insights into what resonates with your customers. Knowing your ICPs and customer personas is a huge help in running geo-targeted display ads within specific geographic areas.

Building engaging ads is a lot easier when you have a clear understanding of who your audiences are, what they want, and why. Your Brand Foundation and Brand Expression work to provide the strategic insights you need to inform and streamline the creative ad development process from both a copywriting and design perspective.

Paid search advertising: Running paid ads on the Google Search Network works well when educated customers are further down the funnel and recognize they have an unavoidable problem. At that point in the buyer's journey, they are actively searching for a solution, hopefully using the benefits and blurbs you defined in your audience and offering messaging outlined in the Backstory Messaging Funnel.

Landing pages: Targeting a specific ICP or customer persona with audience-specific landing pages in response to a customer clicking on a pay-per-click ad can effectively test your messaging to see what resonates with customers and best converts them. Copy for landing pages practically writes itself when you pair benefit headlines and blurbs using the methodology we've discussed.

Social media posts: Creating engaging social media content isn't the first step, but it's an important one. Rather than having a junior team throw ideas and copy against the wall to see what sticks, you can use our methodology to create strategic posts because you already know what resonates and why. You have to monitor and respond to user engagement to grow your following and enhance your authority, but having an intimate understanding of your ICPs and customer personas guides the content creation process and makes better use of the time and talent of your resource-constrained content marketing team.

Content marketing: Developing an integrated content marketing strategy leverages the strengths of all four types of content: paid, earned, shared, and owned (PESO). Building a funnel-based content strategy is a lot easier when you know what to say. It gives you confidence to focus on execution and efficiencies of scale rather than getting bogged down in an endless internal debate.

With the fragmentation of the media landscape and the atomization of content, it takes forethought and coordinated planning to anticipate all the ways content can be repurposed and repackaged. Doing so allows you to maximize your investment in content marketing specific to the unique goals and objectives for each type of content at each stage of the marketing funnel. The Funnel-Based Content Strategy table outlines these interrelated goals and objectives. For the purposes of this table, a trade publication covers the market or industry you work in (where your competitors are), and a vertical publication covers the industries to which you sell.

FUNNEL-BASED CONTENT STRATEGY			
Funnel Stage	TOFU: Top of Funnel	MOFU: Middle of Funnel	BOFU: Bottom of Funnel
Focus	WHAT is happening?	WHY is it happening?	HOW can it be solved?
Types of Content	EARNED MEDIA • Brand messaging • Content others create • Contributed articles (bylines) • Infographics (if good enough) • Story pitches, trend hijacking	OWNED/SHARED MEDIA • Audience and offering messaging • Content you create and share • Blog, community, and social media posts • Infographics and newsletters • Webinars, brand journalism, podcasts	PAID MEDIA • Audience- and offering-specific messaging • Content you create and promote • PPC ads and posts, articles, GIFs, and infographics • Outdoor/print ads, videos
Strategy	Promote the problem: Talk about what's changed and the pain of the same in long-form content.	Define the solution criteria in terms of your unique differentiators.	Explain your solution and how it uniquely satisfies the success criteria in short, easy-to-digest messages.
Types of Narratives	Major data-driven business impact pieces that tie into a financial or popular trend—these stories are high-level and typically demonstrate the financial impact a trend or business is having on the market.	Problem/solution stories that focus on a specific technology or industry—these stories are a bit more technical in nature and demonstrate a problem and either call for or provide a solution.	Typically, but not always, these are case study–driven stories that show how specific technologies or products can impact a particular industry or vertical market.

FUNNEL-BASED CONTENT STRATEGY		
Funnel Stage	**TOFU:** Top of Funnel	**MOFU:** Middle of Funnel	**BOFU:** Bottom of Funnel
Target Publication Examples	Top-tier business or consumer publications: *CNN, USA Today, WSJ, NYT, FT, Fortune, Forbes, Business Insider*	Trade publications or industry newsletters: *eWeek, TechCrunch, Popular Science, WIRED*	Vertical publications that target specific industries: *Nation's Restaurant News, American Banker, Smart Cities Dive, Cyber Defense Magazine*
Marketing Goals	• Build brand awareness • Accelerate funnel • Enable sales/ generate leads • Validate CEO's vision • Bolster customer loyalty • Tell an in-depth version of your story • Establish the five criteria for solving the problem that only you can satisfy	• Funnel acceleration (B2B) • Enable sales/ generate leads • Customer loyalty • Brand awareness	• Enable sales/ generate leads (B2C) • Funnel acceleration • Customer loyalty • Brand awareness

(Source: Created in collaboration with Josh Heath, strategic communications advisor.)

Sales and investor decks: After following the process outlined in this book, decks come together quickly, too, based on the groundwork you've laid, with an emphasis on establishing the prevalence and significance of the problem you solve and your unique five-factor solution to it. For sales and investor decks, remember to keep the amount of information on the slides to a minimum for facilitated presentations. Putting detailed information on slides works for leave-behind versions of your presentations, but having too much text on a slide makes it difficult for audience members to focus on what you're saying because they're preoccupied with reading everything on the screen.

Collateral: Building marketing collateral comes together quickly when you've already got a content library of messaging blocks and messaging stacks from which to pull. Matching the right messages to the right audiences takes just a few minutes because you've already thought through all the details. With clear direction on what to say established, copywriters can focus on how to apply your brand voice to your marketing materials. Your visual brand style guide gives designers the direction they need on the typography, colors, and images to use to create a look and feel that is on brand.

Video: Like marketing collateral, writing scripts for brand and product videos leverages and combines content from your messaging framework, message maps, and brand narrative by combining messaging blocks and stacks. Using AI tools is much easier when you have purely relevant content ingredients, including benefit statements and blurbs, to feed into the automated or semiautomated scriptwriting process. You should never blindly delegate any aspect of the content creation process to an AI tool, but they can accelerate the drafting and iterative creation process when you have quality inputs to feed and fuel their prompts and algorithmic engines.

Trade shows: Brand messaging is an important input to trade show marketing because it communicates who you are and what you do to everyone in attendance at a show at a high level. It's then supported by messages that target specific industries and customer segments in the form of audience-specific presentations, customer case studies, customer testimonials, and collateral. These communication pieces can change from show to show while retaining the brand messaging architecture for the main booth graphics. The combination of brand, audience, and offering messaging makes this more effective and efficient, helping set your brand apart from the sea of sameness within your industry.

Events: Producing events is easier now that you know your audiences and what they care about. Programming content feels intuitive, informed by the structure of your strategic brand narrative and knowing how to bring it to life in ways relevant to each of your customer segments and in keeping with your brand.

Outdoor advertising: Whether online or offline, creating compelling ad campaigns flows directly from your understanding of who buys your products and services and why. Your brand promise and primary and supporting benefits become a source of inspiration for creative copywriters who need to be pointed in the right direction to not only entertain but sell. Your visual design guidelines have already been mapped out so designers know the parameters to work within and which rules they can break without compromising the integrity of your brand.

Brand Activation is a lot more strategic, straightforward, impactful, and fun when it's informed by clearly defined Brand Expression principles and guidelines, which are, in turn, built on a strong, strategic Brand Foundation. Without these foundational guiding principles, the creative and content marketing process can easily veer off course, driven by strong egos, conflicting opinions, misaligned priorities, and attention deficits. If your teams see no one is at the wheel steering your brand toward a defined destination on a well-mapped course, they may wrestle for control and fill the vacuum in a free-for-all that doesn't end well for anyone. It's incredible how much money and time you can waste trying to activate an ill-defined brand no matter how well-meaning your team may be.

Following The Backstory Brand Wheel Framework can help you identify the right audiences and messages to make your marketing dollars work harder for you. Creating cohesive, cogent, consistent brand touch points is vital, but so is defining the right audiences and messages to share with them. It doesn't do your brand or business much good to consistently communicate the wrong messages to the right people and vice versa. You're already spending money on top talent and investing significantly in your go-to-market strategy. Why not make those dollars more impactful with a well-thought-out brand strategy driving them?

CONCLUSION

"I saw the angel in the marble,
and I carved until I set him free."

—Michelangelo

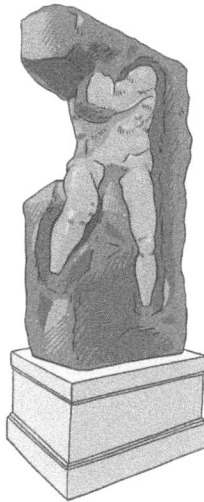

When my wife and I made a bucket list trip to Florence, Italy, we anticipated that seeing *David* by Michelangelo would be one of the trip's highlights. It was. At seventeen feet tall, the larger-than-life statue is more impressive and awe-inspiring than we'd imagined. The corridor leading up to the *David* was surprisingly interesting too. It was lined with a series of unfinished sculptures by Michelangelo.

Art historians refer to these sculptures as "slaves" or stone prisoners because they're trapped in stone, forever frozen, representing different stages of completion. Brands that haven't clarified who they are, what they do, and why it matters are like these unfinished sculptures; we can see glimpses of greatness, but they're stuck in their unfinished state indefinitely.

The purpose of our work at Backstory is to build brands that live up to their promise. Like Michelangelo, our job is to discover and define what is and isn't the essence of a brand and reveal it by removing anything that isn't essential. What our clients receive as a result of this process is pure relevance and resonance with their audiences. What had been an incomplete idea of what they have been or could become is transformed into a clearly defined and refined concept as well as a clearly and consistently communicated idea, story, and relationship that resonates deeply with their ideal customers.

While forming the vision for your organization and developing an effective brand strategy for bringing it to life can be accomplished by a few insightful and passionate leaders, it requires a tremendous amount of insight into who you are as an organization, who your audiences are, what they need, and why. Building out your vision and taking it to market at scale is a team effort that requires the time and talent of many people.

Even Michelangelo worked with a crew of assistants to paint the Sistine Chapel ceiling. They built the scaffolding to put him within arm's reach of the ceiling. They prepared the paint surface, first with a rough coat of plaster followed by a smooth, damp, fine coat of plaster. They mixed the pigments he used with water to make paint. They used paper overlays and charcoal to map out the scenes he painted with full-scale cartoon-like outlines.

Michelangelo may have been the only one holding a paintbrush, but if he had tried to paint the ceiling of the Sistine Chapel by himself, he would have only been able to paint an area about the size of a handkerchief each day because the fresco material had to be damp (it dried out in just an hour or two), and he would have had to mix his own paints.

Other artists in Michelangelo's day struggled to make the studio system work because they chose artisans who lacked the skill to successfully execute their ideas. On a visit to the British Museum, our guide pointed out that certain artists delegated sections of paintings that look decidedly different than the core painting because lesser talents had attempted to fill in those sections. One painting in particular was memorable because the assistants who tried to complete it didn't know how to paint reflections in water. As a result, the painting lacks any reflections for the person walking along the canal or the ducks swimming in it. Choosing the right assistants with the right skill sets and commitment to complement and completely execute your vision to your standards is essential.

Today, artists like Jeff Koons have entire teams that execute his vision in his workshop, or atelier, under his watchful eye, staying true to his brand guidelines and standards. One Koons sculpture can take as many as thirty-three thousand hours to complete. That's just one of hundreds of Koons projects his collective studio is producing simultaneously through this distributed yet consistent approach. Producing multiple works of art on that scale would take too many lifetimes for one artist. Because he has so many ideas and so little time, Koons employs the talents of specialists to bring his visions to life for his creative works, including scientists at MIT and 3D-imaging CAT scan technology. Koons still sees himself as the creator because he designed the systems and processes for bringing his ideas to life in a way consistent with how he would do it if he did everything himself.

This book has provided you with a methodology for bringing your vision to life as you consider what to paint on your brand canvas and sculpt in your studio. You can leverage this process to define your brand and bring it to market at a level that expands your capacity beyond what you can do yourself. With the help of talented teams who follow the process and work within the brand guidelines you've established, the collective work can be true to your standards. The result is a great brand that is bigger than you and your ability to touch every aspect of it—a purposeful brand that can make a difference for good in the world beyond making money.

ACKNOWLEDGMENTS

Writing this book was a cathartic experience, crystallizing concepts my mental rock tumbler has been polishing for years. Sources that have contributed to this process include clients who gave me the opportunity to serve and learn with them; Eric La Brecque for introducing me to the brand wheel concept and being an abundant mentor and friend; Lisa Fortini-Campbell for her mentorship in learning to discover and interpret consumer insights; Nick Copping and Ellie Victor for introducing me to the world of positioning technology companies in the heart of Silicon Valley; Penny March and Jeff Baldwin for teaching me how to write; Mike Thacker and Dave Houle for showing me the power of persistence; Isaac Cloward, Sanja Stanic, and Davor Milanko for their thoughtful feedback and suggestions; my wife, Angie, for her encouragement and support in making time to write; my kids, Maddie, Miranda, Davis, and Sadie Morley—for the unquenchable flame of "Big Guy" love they ignited in me; my parents, Gary and Diane Morley, for their love of reading and example of lifelong learning; and God the Father and His Son, Jesus Christ, for leading me along the way and giving us all the opportunity to fill the measure of our creation.

NOTES

Chapter 2

1. "Prepared for Peace," political ad for Ronald Reagan, October 31, 1984, posted January 4, 2018, by the Museum of Classic Chicago Television, YouTube, https://www.youtube.com/watch?v=KJdDdEa9uXU.

Chapter 3

1. Lisa Baertlein and Terril Yue Jones, "Starbucks Aims to Woo China Workers, Parents," Reuters, April 19, 2023, https://www.reuters.com/article/uk-starbucks-china-employees/starbucks-aims-to-woo-china-workers-parents-idUSLNE83I01H20120419.

2. "What Metrics Matter Most for Saas Companies - Google Search," n.d., https://www.google.com/search?q=what+metrics+matter+most+for+saas+companies&oq=what+metrics+matter+most+for+saas+companies&aqs=chrome..69i57.6640j0j7&sourceid=chrome&ie=UTF-8.

3. See https://styleguide.mailchimp.com.

Chapter 4

1. W. Chan Kim and Renée Mauborgne, *Blue Ocean Strategy: How to Create Uncontested Market Space and Make the Competition Irrelevant* (Harvard Business Review Press, 2015).

2. "A Sunday on La Grande Jatte—1884," Art Institute of Chicago, accessed August 28, 2024, https://www.artic.edu/artworks/27992/a-sunday-on-la-grande-jatte-1884.

3. A. G. Lafley and Roger Martin, *Playing to Win: How Strategy Really Works* (Harvard Business Review Press, 2013), 15.

Chapter 5

1. "The Golden Circle," SimonSinek.com, accessed August 28, 2024, https://simonsinek.com/golden-circle.

2. Roy Spence, *It's Not What You Sell, It's What You Stand For* (Portfolio, 2009), 9–10.

3. Spence, *It's Not What You Sell*, 9–10.

4. Spence, *It's Not What You Sell*, 33.

5. Ryan Sanders, "How Ryan Sanders Co-founded BambooHR," *Utah Business*, November 9, 2023, https://www.utahbusiness.com/how-ryan-sanders-co-founded-bamboohr.

6. Davis Smith, "In the early years of Cotopaxi," LinkedIn, 2022, https://www.linkedin.com/posts/davismsmith_look-out-patagonia-cotopaxi-is-the-colorful-activity-6937046494352998400-2JPW.

7. Steven Bartlett, "Simon Sinek: The Advice Young People NEED To Hear," September 8, 2022, *The Diary of a CEO*, podcast, YouTube, https://www.youtube.com/watch?v=NcaQUH2K-wo.

8. Ryan Peralta, "Thank You COVVI! You Made an Amazing Hand," LinkedIn, accessed December 11, 2024, https://www.linkedin.com/posts/rhp_motivational-speaker-ryan-hudson-peralta-activity-6965711918955192320-j5Y_/.

9. "7 Simple Rules of Brainstorming," IDEO, accessed September 12, 2024, https://www.ideou.com/blogs/inspiration/7-simple-rules-of-brainstorming?srsltid=AfmBOooMIi2-sQGjVT7WeiJbric8F20Vg2PoaD5mwAfrU6l8S2kvNMRM.

10. Barbara Farfan, "Nike's 11 Maxims and Mission Statement," LiveAbout, updated October 9, 2018, https://www.liveabout.com/nike-mission-statement-and-maxims-4138115.

Chapter 6

1. Geoffrey Moore, *Crossing the Chasm* (Harper Collins, 1999), 154.

Chapter 8

1. "9 Surprising Facts About the Tower of London Moat," Historic Royal Palaces, accessed August 30, 2024, https://www.hrp.org.uk/tower-of-london/history-and-stories/9-surprising-facts-about-the-tower-of-london-moat/#gs.69i9zn.

2. "SC Johnson HQ: Exterior and Interior," Frank Lloyd Wright, accessed August 30, 2024, https://www.pbs.org/kenburns/frank-lloyd-wright/sc-johnson-hq-ext-int.

3. Jerry Seinfeld: "10 Things Jerry Seinfeld Can't Live Without," *GQ*, May 1, 2024, https://www.gq.com/video/watch/gq-10-essentials-jerry-seinfeld.

Chapter 9

1. Terry O'Reilly, "Three Foot Marketing," October 7, 2023, *Under the Influence with Terry O'Reilly*, podcast, https://podcasts.apple.com/us/podcast/three-foot-marketing/id493536367?i=1000630546226.

2. "Brand Archetypes," OVO, accessed August 30, 2024, https://brandsbyovo.com/expertise/brand-archetypes.

Chapter 10

1. Ash Maurya, *Running Lean: Iterate from Plan A to a Plan That Works* (O'Reilly Media, Inc. 2012), 27.

2.   Andy Rachleff, "Why You Should Find Product-Market Fit Before Sniffing Around for Venture Money," *Fast Company*, July 25, 2023, https://www. fastcompany.com/3014841/why-you-should-find-product-market-fit-before-sniffing-around-for-venture-money.

3.   Ash Maurya, "10 Steps to Product / Market Fit," presentation at Pioneers Festival, October 2012, YouTube video, https://www.youtube.com/ watch?v=Nhl5nzUNQCA.

4.   Ash Maurya, "How I am Measuring Product/Market Fit," Medium, November 17, 2009, https://medium.com/lean-stack/ how-i-am-measuring-product-market-fit-12db33ef9219.

5.   I'm using the term "offering" here to reference a product or service. Also, we define a solution as an offering that combines a product and service.

Chapter 12

1.   "Glossary," Catchword, accessed September 2, 2024, https:// catchwordbranding.com/glossary.

2.   Ben Gilbert and David Rosenthal, "Costco," August 20, 2023, *Acquired*, podcast, https://www.acquired.fm/episodes/costco.

3.   Mark Pendergast, *For God, Country, and Coca-Cola: The Definitive History of the Great American Soft Drink and the Company That Makes It* (Basic Books, 2013), 28.

4.   Ryan Sanders, "How Ryan Sanders Co-founded BambooHR," *Utah Business*, November 9, 2023, https://www.utahbusiness.com/ how-ryan-sanders-co-founded-bamboohr.

5.   Kate Smith, "Color Symbolism and Meaning of Blue," Sensational Color, August 1, 2020, https://www.sensationalcolor.com/meaning-of-blue.

6.   See https://styleguide.mailchimp.com/voice-and-tone.

7.   James Clear, "Core Values List," JamesClear.com, accessed September 2, 2024, https://jamesclear.com/core-values.

INDEX

H

hard differentiators, 141–42

Harley-Davidson, 140

Hasso Plattner Institute of Design
(d.school), 91

Havenpark Communities, 40–41,
116–18

Hawking, Stephen, 97

Healthcare Information and Management Systems Society
(HIMSS), 47

Heath, Josh, 237

Hero archetype, 143

Hertz, 60

Hess, Garin, 106, 208

Hinckley, Gordon B., 71

Home Depot, 143

Home Improvement (TV series), xiv

"Home to Adventure" tagline, 47

Hormozi, Alex, 129

Houle, Dave (coach), xv

house of brands naming strategy,
205–6

HSBC, 203

Hudson-Peralta, Ryan, 89–90

Human Services HQ, 211

hypergrowth, 13–14. *See also* business
growth

I

ICPs (Ideal Customer Profiles), 165,
176, 185

Ideal Customer Profiles (ICPs), 165,
176, 185

IDEO, xviii, 90–92

IKEA, 203

in-depth interviews, 19–48. *See also*
Brand Discovery

about, 18–23

Brand Ladder Method, 23–28

coding, 43

compared with qualitative methods,
29–30

completing, 43

external, 33–34, 45

guidelines

asking for clarification, 39–41

asking one question at a time, 37

being comfortable with quiet,
36–37

being ready to off-road, 36

being selective, 34

completing five internal and
fifteen external interviews,
33–34

do not correct inconsequential
mistakes, 41

do not settle for saturation, 39

gathering information, 35

getting name and brief bio of
participants, 35

guiding the discussion, 38

pretending to know nothing,
35–36

taking trigger notes, 38–39

tripping over the truth, 45–47

insights from, 47–48

internal, 33–34, 44

modes of, 43–44

ABOUT THE AUTHOR

Photographer: Laura Kinser

JED G. MORLEY is the founder and CEO of Backstory Branding, a brand strategy and messaging consultancy committed to building brands that live up to their promise. Jed has helped dozens of companies get their stories straight so they can scale. He thrives on working with leaders and teams to clarify their purpose, articulate their value, and codify their culture. Jed has a BA in design from Brigham Young University and an MS in Integrated Marketing Communications from Northwestern University. Outside of work, Jed enjoys supporting the performing arts with his wife, Angie; spending time with family; riding his bike; and doing Swedish genealogy.